As her story demonstra⟍ ⟍⟍⟍⟍⟍⟍ ⟍⟍⟍ ⟍⟍⟍⟍⟍⟍
ing - and challenging o⟍ ⟍⟍⟍⟍⟍⟍⟍⟍⟍⟍⟍⟍ ⟍⟍⟍⟍ ⟍⟍⟍ ⟍⟍⟍⟍⟍ ⟍⟍⟍
where, at any cost. This book tells the moving and challenging
story of Mrs. B's faithful service over six decades. The course of
her life, from a farm girl from Saskatchewan to a widow in Panama to a beloved missions teacher and sought-after conference
speaker, has tested her resolve, and proven God's faithfulness.
This book will make you cry, rattle your complacency, and remind you that God wants all of you. It is a book I want my kids
to read, so they know they can trust God with their zip code.

*Jon Arnold, Counselor (Development) Canadian High
Commission in Tanzania. Mrs. B.'s Former Teaching assistant*

This is an incredible journey. The young lady could never have
imagined what it might mean when she signed her name on a
card with the simple commitment, "Anywhere, Any Time, Any
Cost." I have always admired Jean Barsness, but now that I have
read her life story, I am even more deeply impressed with this
amazing woman. God led her from remote Canadian prairies
to bustling Panama City, then on to the mountains of Ecuador,
and finally back to where it all started. This author's unwavering
trust is inspiring. God's unfailing grace is encouraging. Once
you start reading this book, you won't want to put it down.

*Dr. Ron Blue, Former President of CAM (Camino Global)
and Professor at Dallas Theological Seminary*

More than anyone, it was Jean Barsness whom God used to en-
large my worldview as I sat in her Missions class at Briercrest
Bible College in 1985. Other students experienced a similar
transformation in knowing God's heart for the world He loves,
and being ignited to a deeper commitment to serving Him.

Reading the story I only thought I knew, has enriched my understanding of this woman's impact on my life. A new generation of Kingdom builders needs to learn from her example.

Moira Brown, CoHost of 100 Huntley Street on CTS TV

The work of God down through the centuries is made up of millions of intertwined stories; stories of God's grace expressed through people. Jean's story is a powerful reminder that the glory of God is manifest through people who listen and walk in obedience to Him. *Anywhere...Anytime...Any Cost* is a call to embrace all God has for us and join Him in the grand adventure of life, regardless of the zip code.

Charles A. Cook, PhD
Professor of Global Studies and Mission (Ambrose University
College) Chair, Global Mission Roundtable (EFC)

INTEGRITY! Jean Barsness has it. In this book, Jean Barsness lets her life speak a life wholly abandoned to God. Anyone who wants to know more about the surrendered life will want to read this compelling story - now.

Gordon Elhard, Founding Member of Calgary Centre Street
Church. High School Principal and School Superintendent

This book is not just an interesting story. It's the intriguing journey of a woman who has lived life to the full through obedience in following God. Her journey has had twists and turns, potholes, speed bumps, and even its share of crashes, but through it all she has experienced God's love and learned to trust His goodness and faithfulness. Jean's story provides a road map for your journey at whatever stage of the trip you find yourself.

Rosemary Flaaten, M.A. Best Selling Author,
Speaker and Life Coach.
www.rosemaryflaaten.com

This story is the powerful testimony of a woman's life completely surrendered to God. Through tragedy and triumph, the pages resound with the truth of God's faithfulness. Dr. Barsness yielded her life to the Lordship of Jesus Christ, and He provided for her. Truly, her story is an example to us all!

Cindy Klassen, Six-time Canadian Olympic Medalist

God, who is sovereign and faithful, will work out His purposes for His honour and glory! Dr. Jean Barsness' story humbly and decisively directs us to this truth that God is completely trustworthy and His timing perfect. We are deeply challenged to surrender everything to Him and truly trust Him with our Zip Code because that is the best possible place to be!

Rev. Phil Ruten, President of Millar College of The Bible

Jean's story is full of practical insights and exciting stories of how a young women followed God to the mission field, experienced fruit and tragedy which continued to build a clear unmistakable commitment to Christ. Jean has had an impact on a generation of Canadian young men and women, who were challenged and motivated by her teaching and life, many of whom today are serving all over the world.

Dr, Frank M. Severn, Director Emeritus, Send International

A remarkable narrative this - nothing less than a moving account of God at work, shaping a beautiful Masterpiece. One decision in July, 1949 changed not only Jean Little's eternal destiny but her entire life. She grappled with the personal implications of becoming a Christ follower. Then, she was ready and decided - Jesus is my Lord! Anywhere, Anytime, Any Cost!

God took her up on it! That incredible story is now told and must be read, for it glorifies God and challenges all of us to be more than just "cultural Christians," or even " fans " of Jesus, when we too could find fulfillment as Biblical Christ followers.

Dr. Neil Snider, President Emeritus
Trinity Western University

Attending Candidate Orientation Program together in 1954, Jean became the youngest missionary to be appointed and licensed with the Gospel Missionary Union. You will be greatly enriched by her missionary experiences and her account of a very rich life of walking with the Lord through trials and difficulties which allowed God the Father through His loving care and discipline to mold her into one of the leading missionary personalities of our time.

Rev. Jim Taylor, Former Vice President for Europe and Africa
for AVANT Ministries

Since I first met Jean as my missions teacher at Briercrest 30 years ago, she has been a profound encourager in my life; helping me to see the Father's heart for our world and to understand His mandate to make disciples. This book sets the context of a life given to pointing people to the Father; teaching, modeling, and encouraging people to make Jesus the Lord of their life. For the sake of the gospel, Jean has been one to obey her Lord, and care for people. In this book Jean asks and answers the question we all must ask 'is God trustworthy with our life' – one hundred times yes!

Dr. Dwayne Uglem, President Emeritus of Briercrest College and Seminary

This is what our generation needs, real stories of real people and real places, experiencing the presence and power of God. Be ready to be challenged as you read Jean Barsness story.

Rev. Galo Vasquez, Director of Latin American Ministries: Billy Graham Evangelistic Association

ANYWHERE,
ANYTIME,
ANY COST

Can I trust GOD with my zip code?

To Dorothy...
With gratitude for
your friendship and
encouragement.
2 Cor. 4:5,7

Foreword by Col. Al Romaneski,
Former Chief of the Western Hemisphere Division OJCS in the Pentagon

ANYWHERE, ANYTIME, ANY COST

Can I trust GOD with my zip code?

A. Jean Barsness

ANYWHERE, ANYTIME, ANY COST
Copyright © 2013 by A. Jean Barsness

Scripture quotations marked "KJV" are taken from the Holy Bible, King James Version, Cambridge, 1769. • Scripture quotations marked "NASB" are taken from the NEW AMERICAN STANDARD BIBLE®, Copyright © 1960, 1962, 1963, 1968, 1971, 1972, 1973, 1975, 1977, 1995 by The Lockman Foundation. Used by permission. • Scripture quotations marked "NIV" are taken from THe HOLY BIBLE, NEW INTERNATIONAL VERSION®, NIV® Copyright © 1973, 1978, 1984, 2011 by Biblica, Inc.™ Used by permission. All rights reserved worldwide. • Scripture quotations marked "NKJV" are taken from the New King James Version / Thomas Nelson Publishers, Nashville: Thomas Nelson Publishers, Copyright © 1982. Used by permission. All rights reserved. • Scripture quotations marked "NLT" are taken from the Holy Bible, New Living Translation, copyright 1996. Used by permission of Tyndale House Publishers, Inc., Wheaton, Illinois 60189. All rights reserved. • Scripture quotations marked "Phillips" are taken from The New Testament in Modern English, copyright © 1958, 1959, 1960 J.B. Phillips and 1947, 1952, 1955, 1957 The Macmillian Company, New York. Used by permission. All rights reserved.

Printed in Canada

ISBN: 978-1-4866-0122-6

Word Alive Press
131 Cordite Road, Winnipeg, MB R3W 1S1
www.wordalivepress.ca

Cataloguing in Publication may be obtained through Library and Archives Canada

Dedicated with much love and appreciation
to my twin sister
Joan
whose Irish wit, love for the Scriptures,
profound faith and faithful prayers
have been a constant encouragement,
inspiration and blessing.

Contents

Acknowledgements

THIS MANUSCRIPT WOULD NOT HAVE BEEN WRITTEN HAD IT NOT BEEN FOR THE encouragement of many who motivated me to go beyond my comfort zone and trust God to enable me to do what humanly I could not. Without their phone calls, visits and inspiring notes, the first sentence would not have been typed.

Within one week, God confirmed that telling my story was His plan. He used Apple Creative Craig Learmont, encouraged me to buy a laptop, put my feet up and start writing. Rosemary Flaaten promised to keep me accountable. Gratitude fills my heart for Dave and Lorraine Anderson, Wynn and Gordon Lautermilch and Faith Nixdorff, who have graciously helped with the publication of my manuscript. An unexpected call from Moira Brown of CTS's 100 Huntley Street urged me to start writing.

My thanks to those who have provided information and personal accounts to be inserted in the text. Thank you Vange Doerksen, Noreen Klassen, Eduardo and Aggie Mellado, Gene McIntosh, Leander Rempel, Joan Diener, Abilio Fernandez and Marilyn Romaneski. Marilyn assured me that she would be the first to read my book. I didn't finish in time. God took my dear friend Marilyn Home just weeks before the manuscript was completed.

Many thanks to Kathy Covert for her encouragement to write my story and for the hours spent editing the story. Thanks to Tim Lenko for his inspiration and skilled help. I am so indebted to Murray Arnold, who offered to edit and check punctuation within the manuscript. Thank you Murray for hours reading papers again, this time mine.

Thanks to my children, Glen and Betts, for taking the painful step of reliving their father's death and writing their impressions and responses to Christ in a time of crisis.

I am so grateful to God for Dr. Enrique and Alice Chi, Dr. Abilio Fernandez, Mary Saenz and many others in Panama who in my recent visit to Panama, reviewed paragraphs that related to the crisis in Panama and prompted me to recount some events that would probably not have been included apart from their encouragement.

My thanks to my husband, Alton, who was a continual inspiration and encouraged me to persevere when I became weary in well doing and was ready to pack it all in.

Many thanks for the joy of partnering with Tiffany, Kylee, Larissa and the staff of WORD ALIVE PRESS for their encouragement, inspiration and skilled assistance in publishing my story.

Profound gratitude goes to my Heavenly Father for pursuing me with His love, giving daily strength and reminding me of stories of His provision and direction. Without Him, there would not be a story. It is a story of His amazing grace.

Preface

SIX DECADES AGO. IT SEEMS SO LONG . . . AND YET, HARDLY YESTERDAY. I STOOD IN a Bible college gymnasium, only a teenager, faced with a choice. Could I really trust God with my zip code? That missions conference was the tool God used to show me the reality of His Lordship. I was reluctant to surrender, but still I scribbled my signature on a card that read "Anywhere, Anytime, Any Cost." They were the words of determination and devotion from the heart of a teenager. I meant every word, but I had absolutely no idea of the implications.

One evening at the conference, I crossed the line from a believer to a follower, making a public declaration that I would relinquish my dreams and personal plans to tuck in close behind Him to walk by faith into the unknown. I had no idea what radical abandonment to God might look like. Walking by faith is like that.

Stories become illustrations of how God blesses, guides, provides and shows Himself strong to those who relinquish all to follow Him in obedience. I discovered that each day became a reason to celebrate. As I began to write, God was evident in each story.

As I have trusted Jesus, He has taken me places I would never have dreamt. He has given me more years to serve than ever expected. He has enabled me to do more than I ever could imagine. This is my story, from the Canadian prairies to the high-rises and beaches of Panama, to the majestic Andes Mountains of Ecuador and back to where it all began.

The words of Beth Maxfield (now Beth Ashabraner) resonate as she beautifully conveys the reality that we are all alike and all are on a journey:

> I am just like you. I am created, cherished, claimed and chosen. My soiled soul, like yours, has been washed sparkling clean in His living water. I, like you, am not my own; I am His. I, like you, have embarked on a spiritual sojourn . . . one that has led me across seas, through valleys, over mountains. I rejoice, as you do, in a Savior who took the time to grip the pen of grace and scribble this rugged story of redemption . . . my story.[1]

As a teenager, I said an overwhelming "Yes" to God. I, too, have handed Him my pen, and I have asked Him to write my story.

It is a story of His amazing grace. I desire to showcase God and illustrate from six decades as a Christ follower that He is unreservedly trustworthy and deserving of our radical abandonment to Him.

Each of us has a story to tell. This is mine . . .

---

[1] Bethany Maxfield, "A Savior's Scribbles," Missions Publication of the Church of God Vol. 66 No 5 (September/October 2002). For more of Beth's writing, you may visit her blog at www.bethanyashabraner.com.

Foreword

JEAN BARSNESS'S *ANYWHERE, ANYTIME, ANY COST* IS THE STORY OF GOD'S FAITHFUL provision in her life told through the framework of the amazing events of her life. The title could well have been "God's Story" or "Jehovah Jireh" or "Sacrifices on the Altar" or "Stayed Upon Jehovah" or any number of other titles. Whatever the title, this true story is one of powerful, gripping events orchestrated by a faithful God to bring blessing into the author's life and glory to His Kingdom.

When Jean asked my opinion about whether she should write an account about her life, I was very enthusiastic about the project. I believed that it would be a marvelous reference and legacy for her family and friends. Now her effort has produced an entire book that will be a broader inspiration to countless readers beyond her inner circle. This book has the power to change your attitude about how to be obedient to God and how to trust Him.

The centerpiece of *Anywhere, Anytime, Any Cost* is the brutal, tragic murder of Jean's husband, Gil Reimer, in Panama. It was a truly tragic loss for all of us who knew and loved this kind, gentle man. Death separated Gil from us in this world and deprived us of the fellowship of a giant of the faith. Gil was murdered though he had done no wrong nor was any deceit in his mouth, and "tragic" seems to be the appropriate adjective to use concerning this terrible event, even though God has used it to influence many of us to renew our total commitment to God's work. The stab wounds in Gil's body remind us of the suffering of our

Lord Jesus on the cross, and like Jesus, Gil may have been betrayed by a friend—the man in the suit.

Gil was a martyr for the Gospel. We ordinarily think of martyrdom as suffering unto death for the sake of one's faith, However the Greek word *martys* means "witness." Gil in his short life was a powerful living witness to the lifestyle and to the walk in life of the devoted Christ follower, whether or not facing death. Who knows how many lives have responded positively to God's grace because of the example of Gil's life and steadfast witness?

Gil's memorial service in Panama was a victory celebration! To this day, the hymn "Like a River Glorious" evokes deep emotion and tears because it was one of the musical praises at Gil's memorial service at Crossroads Church in Panama. Recalling the words "Stayed upon Jehovah, hearts are fully blest, finding as He promised perfect peace and rest" reminds me of the hundreds of Americans and Panamanians—brothers and sisters in Christ—gathered within the church and on the grounds outside the church to pay tribute to Gil's memory and to his victorious life.

A particularly poignant part of the book refers to placing cherished parts of one's life on altars of offering and thanks before the Lord. It is a deliberate decision based on trust to surrender to God's will in all things: Anywhere, Anytime, Any Cost. Just as Abraham erected an altar to Yahweh at Bethel, we can offer life's treasures on an altar to God; in Jean's case—vocation, singleness, children.

This book is a life changer. The reader cannot come away without having his emotions touched and his faith strengthened. When we read how God sovereignly provided for the author and her small children in very special and intimate ways, our faith is strengthened. Just one of many examples is how God relocated two American families from Panama to Quito, Ecuador, ahead of Jean, so that they were already there to welcome her and care for her when Jean and her children arrived.

Emotionally, sadness about Gil turns to joy as God continues to bless the author and to use her in a number of important ministries. The last line rings true: "The final chapter has yet to be written," because Jean continues to serve the Lord faithfully Anywhere, Anytime, Any Cost, and God still has the pen.

Submitted by
Col. Al Romaneski, Former Chief of the Western Hemisphere Division OJCS in the Pentagon.

June 8, 2013

Family History

My Heritage: One Hundred Percent Irish
I AM THE DAUGHTER OF AN IMMIGRANT.

Matthew Henry Little, my dad, was born in Sligo, Ireland, one of three children. His only brother, Joseph, was killed in World War I. He had one sister, Sadie. His mom, Joanna Gillespie Little, was a noted and gifted speaker, and traveled throughout the United Kingdom. Although she was a very humble Christian woman, she dined with the elite. Like his mom, Dad's first cousin Greta Cousins was a speaker and champion for rights. Greta and her husband moved to India, where she continued being an advocate for women, becoming the First Lady Magistrate in India.

As Dad and his two cousins approached their twenties, adventure was in their bones. They began to plan for a voyage to Canada. "Should we sail from Liverpool in March or in April?"

The decision was made. They would book a transatlantic passage on the SS Caledonia for March 1912, third class. When I asked my dad why third class, he replied, "Because there wasn't a fourth." Had they decided to sail one month later, they would have been on the Titanic! If that had been the case, there would not be a story to tell. God was in this decision.

Unlike Dad's family, mom was raised amongst a bustling bunch of thirteen siblings. Her father, David (Dub) Mayne, had also been born in Ireland and immigrated to Canada. He became a member of the North West Mounted Police, stationed on the Montana/Saskatchewan border.

David was known for his adventurist spirit. His career was rife with intrigue and exploit. At the turn of the century he married Deborah Jones from Winchester, Indiana, and together they pioneered on the Canadian prairies.

Following a year in the Toronto area, Dad moved west and homesteaded in southern Saskatchewan. While attending church one Sunday, he met Elizabeth Mayne. Everyone knew them as "Harry and Liz."

They were married when Dad was thirty-two and Mom was nineteen. Immediately after their wedding in Woodrow, Saskatchewan, Harry and Liz sailed to Ireland, where they would spend one year. Mom loved the Emerald Isle but was resigned and ready for her humble homestead in southern Saskatchewan.

My Home: The Saskatchewan Prairies

I recall stories mom told us of those initial homestead days. They themselves marveled at their courage, faith and resourcefulness as early pioneers. She remembered well the loneliness of a prairie homesteader's life and how they faced one crisis after another. She recalled how, within one year, their firstborn son was caught in a thrashing machine, their home was destroyed by fire and hail totally wiped out any possibility of a harvest.

"Well, every Little bit helps!" was Harry Little's response on becoming the father of twin daughters. After three boys, he was overjoyed with girls, and two of them! It was a stormy January day in Kincaid, Saskatchewan, when my "womb mate" and I entered the world. Little we were, as we arrived unexpectedly two months early. "Little" in name and definitely in size, we weighed in just over four pounds each.

Our mom had decided on names. Mom's beloved friend and nurse, Miss Glen, had other plans. She was definite that we "looked like a Jean and Joan." Mom's nurse named us and those names stuck. Mom's choices went by the wayside and we became Audrey Joanna and Aileen Jean. For all our lives we have been called by our middle names—interesting thing to do to a child!

As one gets older it becomes even more confusing. Documents always seem to need an explanation.

Right from the beginning we were a team. Our two older brothers were convinced that we were terribly spoiled. There were times a spanking was deserved but avoided. One of those instances was an attempt to visit a friend.

Even little four-year-old girls know that "two can accomplish more than one," especially if there is a plan, a plan to accomplish a common goal. We wanted to test our strategy. Our dad had bought a Model T Ford and it was parked in front of the house. We had a vision. We had a plan. We had a purpose. We loved Blanch and we decided to visit her.

If we worked as a team, surely we could drive the black Model T to Blanch's house. The plan seemed sound. One twin would crouch on the car floor, working brakes, and gas. The other would sit on the seat and manage the steering wheel. The plan worked all the way down the long driveway, but then we had a wee problem. We couldn't make the turn at the main road and we landed in the potato patch, stuck, good and proper!

Years later Joan and I heard our brothers say, "And they didn't even get spanked."

This was the beginning of many an adventure and challenge. There would be more potato patches!

With lunch buckets in hand at age five and a half, Joan and I trudged off for a one-mile walk to begin our academic journey with Bob and David, our two older brothers, protecting us and Brian, our younger brother.

As a young teenager, oratory and public speaking totally intrigued me, so much so that I always applied to participate in oratory contests. So fascinated was I with the public speaking skills of Saskatchewan's Premier Tommy Douglas, that I would beg my dad to let me accompany him to any political meetings where Tommy Douglas would powerfully address large audiences. I did not want to miss even one of his political speeches. I am sure I was the only child in attendance! Bless Dad, he always took me.

Both our parents had a strong faith, work ethic and a vigorous commitment to the Bible, to tithing and to the church. Dad's life was also characterized by generosity. Mom and Dad had an oak hutch, dining room table, and six chairs with leather seats, paying a total of twenty-five dollars for everything. When I was a teenager, I complained to my dad about such old furniture! I compared our old dining room furniture to the new and beautiful furniture owned by the Mennonite neighbors, which prompted an earful from Dad. He said, "As long as this table is useable, we will keep it and give our money to missions." End of discussion! Guess who has this "old" furniture in her dining room today?

Dad kept an old cigar box in the top drawer of the dresser in their bedroom. Whenever a minister of the Gospel enjoyed the hospitality of my parents, very few, if any, left without cash secretly squeezed into his hand. As a child who experienced the depression and terrible dust storms of the 1930s, I knew we were not poor or needy. How could we be? Dad was always giving money away. Our parents modeled what it was to love the Lord with all our heart, to love one another and love our neighbor as ourselves.

I am so thankful for my heritage and for my home. A quote by Donna Hedges expresses it well, "Having a place to go is home. Having someone to love is a family. Having both is a blessing."[2]

Jane Howard concludes, "Call it a clan, call it a network, call it a tribe, call it a family. Whatever you call it, whoever you are, you need one."[3]

[2] Publication source unknown.
[3] Jane Howard, "In Search of the Good Family" in Renée H. Shea, Lawrence Scanlon, and Robin Dissin Aufses, *The Language of Composition: Reading, Writing and Rhetoric* (Boston, MA: Bedford/St. Martin's, 2008), 283-88.

Choices and Commitment as a Teenager

Conversion to Christ

WE GREW UP IN A HOME WHERE THE BIBLE WAS REVERED AND HONORED. FOLLOWING breakfast each morning—guests or no guests—Dad, in his Irish accent, would say, "Get down the Book." He would read from the Scriptures, then we would all kneel for prayer around the kitchen table.

That is how we began each day at the "Little Farm." It is also how we ended our day—on our knees. I clearly recall seeing my father kneel by his bed to pray at the end of each day.

Joan and I shared a bedroom down the hall. Each night my mom would come in to pray with us, as Joan and I would kneel by our bed and recite…

Now I lay me down to sleep
I pray Thee, Lord, my soul to keep
And if I should die before I wake
I pray Thee, Lord, my soul to take.

One might think that this is a very simple prayer. Simple, perhaps, but definitely profound. The words had a lasting affect on my heart and mind. Every night I would crawl into bed with death on my mind. Why wouldn't I?

"If I should die before I wake," was constantly in my thoughts. As a five-year-old, I was terrified with the thought of death. I knew without a doubt that my parents were ready to meet God, but I also knew that I definitely was not.

A Scripture plaque on our kitchen wall also kept before me the need to give my heart to Him. It read, *"Seek ye the Lord while He is near, call ye upon Him while He may be found."* (KJV) Isaiah 55:6 is forever embedded in my mind and heart.

We regularly attended youth meetings at the local Meyronne United Church. I vividly recall one meeting so different from the norm. A handsome older teenager came from a nearby town and shared his story. He explained how he had received the gift of God's grace and salvation through Jesus and had become a Christian. He assured us that he knew where he was going when he died. As a fourteen-year-old, I don't know if I was more impressed with how handsome he was or with his story. I wondered, "How can such a handsome guy have the courage to tell anyone that he is a Christian?"

I am in awe of an Almighty Creator God who is passionate about a relationship with us, so much so that He woos and draws us to Himself. In reality Christianity is the only religious belief system in the world where God initiates the relationship. God loved my sister and me so much that He used a small bedtime prayer, a plaque on the kitchen wall and the testimony of a young man to draw us to His heart. At an early age God created a spiritual vacuum in our hearts and we yearned to know Him.

Perhaps the most powerful instrument that God employed was the ongoing and continual prayers of my parents. The intercession of my mom and dad, with their deep concern for the salvation of their children, was a powerful instrument in the hands of a gracious God. Even in the context of our teenage years, when temptations increased, their prayers escalated.

At the age of fifteen my sister and I attended family camp with our brother. On the last night of camp, the evangelist led the congregation in an old hymn, "Be in time, the Master calls, be in time." I was under incredible conviction, but I resisted through five verses. My feet were glued to the sawdust floor. On the last chorus I reluctantly went to the altar. Quietly I repented, confessed my sins and received the gift of salvation Jesus offered. As I arose from my knees that Sunday night and walked back to my seat, I knew without a doubt that I was His child

On Monday morning I opened my Bible. I had read the Bible before, but this time it was different. My eyes fell on 2 Corinthians 5:17, *"If any man be in Christ, he is a new creature: old things have passed away; behold, all things are become new"* (KJV). The words were alive. It was July 19, 1949. One decision had changed not only my eternal destiny, but also my entire life.

Junior and Senior High School: On a Christian Campus

The high school in our local town was closing, so our parents prepared to send my twin sister and me to Caronport, a Christian high school. It was an incredible sacrifice on their part!

Only six weeks old in Jesus, we found ourselves on a Christian campus where we attended chapels each weekday morning and twice on Sunday. We were immersed in solid biblical teaching from the outset of our walk with Christ. A transformation continued as we absorbed truth and sought purpose.

Although there were many rules, they were not unlike the routine we had at home. At home we had "chores." On campus we had "gratis shift work." The privilege of attending a Christian residential high school was formative in my Christian walk, and I will always be grateful for parents who sacrificed financially in order for my sister and I to attend.

Post Secondary Education: My Way or His?

As a little girl I wanted to be a nurse. The early desire sprouted because of a picture on our piano. My cousin had graduated from nursing school. Her portrait was beautiful. The white nurse's uniform and cap and the dozen roses impressed me. My desire to be a nurse was not based on spiritual gifting or natural abilities like I saw in my mom, who was a "natural" when it came to caring for the sick. She was "at home" in any hospital. I just wanted to make my mom proud.

After graduating from high school I applied for Nurses Training but was rejected because of my age. Seventeen was too young. I had a year to kill. What better place to kill a year than on a Bible college campus?

It would be a perfect context for socializing. I applied to Briercrest Bible Institute and was accepted. I had a plan—it would be one year and no more.

Dad promised to pay for only my first year of schooling. After that I would need to work and pay my own way. I calculated—work for a summer, attend Bible school for one year and then resume the pursuit and dream of nursing. I completed my one year at Briercrest and now I needed a job.

Each summer the Riverview Hospital (Essondale) located in Port Coquitlam, British Columbia, employed college students, and I was fortunate enough to be one of the thirty-two hired. Travel plans were made. I was about to leave home to work for the first time. The prospect of a long train ride from Moose Jaw to Vancouver was terrifying. I didn't fear the journey as much as I feared my potential cabin companion. I had a ticket for the upper berth. Who, just who, would be on the bottom? Worry rattled my bones and consumed my thoughts.

I will never forget the hours of the night before. I committed my fears to God. I knelt by my bed and prayed honestly and specifically. I had no idea who might occupy the berth below. Could I trust him or her? How would I ever be at ease stuck on the top? My prayer was specific. Please provide a Christian woman as a travel mate for two days and two nights. Amen and Amen.

When I boarded the train the next morning and took my seat, I saw evidence of a traveling companion! Whoever it might be, he or she had stepped off the train for a few minutes. Making sure that no one was watching, I began to rummage. Amongst the belongings on the seat beside me was a Bible! My heart soared! I took the liberty to check the name on the front page.

Before my mystery seat partner returned, everything was back in place. My plea had been answered above and beyond imagination. Seated next to me was a missionary returning from Nigeria, about to begin her furlough. God had, indeed, inclined His ear to me and answered my prayer. The faith of a teenage girl right off the farm and on her way to the city was rooted, ever more deeply, in the care of a faithful Savior.

Lessons in obedience awaited this naïve teenager. Rules for Essondale staff in residence were strict. We understood that there would be absolutely no hitch hiking and no one was to leave the campus alone—ever!

It was Sunday afternoon. My shift had ended at three o'clock. I desperately wanted to attend church that evening in New Westminster. I knew the rules. I could not go out alone. A companion must be found. At the Nurse's Residence pay phone I began dialing number after number. Some friends had other plans for the evening. Others simply did not answer.

While I was dialing there was a quiet urging and stirring in my heart. I sensed God telling me to walk down the hall and knock on the door of an elderly lady (she might have been merely in her forties!) God was prompting me to invite her to accompany me to church. When one is eighteen and a person might be forty, there is a wide age gap. I had met the woman just once in the resident kitchen. I did not know her name, although there had probably been an occasional subsequent greeting. I had no idea if she was a believer or not. Did she ever attend church? I ignored the urging and just kept dialing.

Finally, in desperation, I hung up the phone and reluctantly headed down the hall. With fear and intimidation, I knocked. She did not come to the door. She simply answered, "Come in."

"Will you go to church with me tonight?" I blurted. The woman didn't reply. She began to weep. With tears streaming down her face, she explained, "I have been sitting here, asking God to send someone with whom I might attend church tonight."

I couldn't believe it! I was the answer to her prayer. That night, I began to grow in amazement of who Jesus is. He is the Lord who directs steps. He said, *"I will instruct you and teach you in the way you should go; I will counsel you with my loving eye on you"* (Psalm 32:8, NIV). Ours is to obey. I was given a glimpse of God's blessing when I responded in obedience to His gentle urging.

God's Call: To Follow Him

My year was up and my summer employment had ended. Now I could do what I wanted.

The problem was that during that year at Briercrest I began to grapple with the Lordship of Jesus Christ and the personal implications of becoming a Christ follower. As I was presented with the claims of Christ my thoughts were taken captive. The significance of becoming a devoted follower of Jesus Christ filled my mind. In reality, it was terrifying. I thought that if I once surrendered everything to Jesus, He would ask me to become a single lady missionary. If there was any one thing that I did not want to be, it was a single missionary. That would be the death knell for any eventual marriage!

It had been more than two years since I put my trust in the Lord for salvation. I thanked Him for Calvary. I was not worthy of the nail prints in His hands. I was confident that I was His child. But as His child, I wanted my own way. I wanted to write my own story.

Attending chapels five times a week, I was well aware of the implications of following Christ fully. I was also cognizant that Jesus did not hide the cost involved. I knew the pertinent verses related to discipleship. Was I content with being just a believer, not a disciple? Was I satisfied with being a fan and not a follower? How could I ever trust God with my zip code? I had read the book of Luke. Jesus explained the cost to the disciples, and as He talked to the multitudes said,

If anyone comes to Me and does not hate his father and mother, wife and children, brothers and sisters, yes, and his own life also, he cannot be My disciple. And whoever does not bear his cross and come after Me cannot be my disciple. . . . So likewise, whoever of you does not forsake all that he has cannot be My disciple. (Luke 14: 26–27, 33, NKJV)

Jesus was explicit. If I was not willing to die every day—if I was not willing to leave my family in Saskatchewan, if I was not willing to give up everything—then I must not call myself a follower. I was only a believer. Obedience was imperative, for Jesus also said, "But why do you call me 'Lord, Lord,' and not do the things which I say?" (Luke 6:46, NKJV).

These verses were exactly the reason that I grappled and struggled. I reviewed the conditions made clear by Jesus and then asked myself, "Am

I content with just being a believer? Is the cost of being a disciple too great?" I knew the cost of following. Jesus required everything, for He had not kept it a secret. Fear filled my heart.

I also knew Christ's "hundred-fold promise of obedience." I personally pondered His promise and I paraphrased Mark, chapter ten: "I say to you Jean, if you leave your home on the farm, your three brothers and your twin sister, your Irish father and mother and Canada for my sake and the sake of the Gospel, you shall receive a hundredfold now in this time, houses and brothers and sisters and mothers and children and lands, with persecutions . . . and in the age to come, eternal life."

Reflecting on the fear that consumed me, I began to realize that my God-view was entirely flawed and unbiblical. I could not possibly imagine that God's plan could be better than the plan I construed. I could not grasp the truth of an all-loving God giving me gifts, abilities and personality traits that He wanted to use for His glory. How incredibly foolish to think that I could do better!

Immediately following my first year of Bible school, I followed the Lord in the waters of baptism. Being baptized was an act of obedience. While serving as a counselor at the CSSM camp at Arlington Beach in Saskatchewan, I asked the CSSM Director, Rev. Elmer Snider, if he would baptize me. A date was set and Mr. Snider baptized me along with several others one afternoon.

I had just made a public declaration to become a Christ follower. I had crossed the line from a believer to a follower. As I came up out of the waters of Last Mountain Lake, Saskatchewan, everyone on the beach was singing. I was dripping wet but I joined them, singing,

"I have decided to follow Jesus, no turning back, no turning back.

If none go with me, still I will follow, no turning back, no turning back.

The cross before me, the world behind me, no turning back, no turning back."

I was very sincere, but I had no idea of the significance of being a Christ follower, no idea of what that journey would look like. I had no idea of the bumps or potholes in the road. I had no idea of the personal cost or what that might look like. I had made my decision. I had crossed the line. There would be no turning back. The first step after my total surrender to the Lordship of Christ, was to return to Briercrest.

It was in second year of Bible school, during the fall missionary conference, that I made a second public declaration. Dr. T. J. Bach, director of TEAM (The Evangelical Alliance Missions), was the keynote speaker. He was an elderly man with a powerful message. He gave his text, John 15:16. He read, "Jesus said, 'Ye have not chosen me, but I have chosen you and I have ordained you that ye should go and bear fruit.' "

I thought that I had done all the deciding. I believed that the decision was mine and mine alone. Dr. Bach explained that Jesus had made a decision. He had chosen. He had set apart. He had appointed. The apostle Paul further explained, *"We are His workmanship, created in Christ Jesus for good works, which God prepared beforehand that we should walk in them"* (Ephesians 2:10 NKJV).

That night is still clearly etched in my heart and mind because it was that night that I yielded everything to the purposes of God. I stood to my feet, and with radical abandonment to Christ, I wrote my signature on a small card that said, "Anywhere, Anytime, Any Cost." As I yielded control to His will and plan, I gave Him the permission to roll up His sleeves, as it were, to direct my steps and bless me. In almost six decades as a Christ Follower, my life has been enriched and blessed beyond any hopes, dreams and expectations.

God's Calling: To Cross-Cultural Ministry

It was a Sunday evening service and I was now in my third and final year at Briercrest. Dr. Don P. Shidler, President of the Gospel Missionary Union, was the speaker.

Dr. Shidler told of a return flight to Kansas City from Ecuador when mechanical problems interrupted his Braniff Airlines schedule, making necessary a substantial layover in Panama. With time to wander the streets, Dr. Shidler asked many questions and made many observations. It seemed to him that Panama was the Shanghai of Latin America—industrial prosperity at its perimeter, poverty of heart at its interior. Panama, where the party begins and does not end. Panama, the bridge to the Americas. He enquired about the mission organizations working in Panama, only to discover that the majority had established educational institutions. Very few were planting churches. Dr. Shidler's heart was touched and he became burdened for Panama. With obvious zeal, he told us more. Panama, a small country in the shape of a lazy "S," had a population of less than a million. Joining Costa Rica in Central America and Colombia in South America, Panama was pivotal politically and geographically. After much prayer and consultation, it was decided that GMU's next foray would be into this crossroads, this potential Gospel springboard between two continents—Panama.

Dr. Shidler looked at his audience that evening and asked, "Is there anyone in this chapel that would be willing to be a pioneer church planter in Panama?" I was only nineteen years of age, but God began to tug at my heart. I wondered, might this be His calling on my life? The following day the Holy Spirit prompted me to ask for an appointment with Dr. Shidler. The encounter landed me smack in the path of the Gospel Missionary Union as I was handed an application for a missionary career in Panama.

A few months later, I put the completed application in a large manila envelope addressed and ready to mail. Probably the longest trip I have ever taken was the walk from my dorm to the campus post office. With every step, I thought to myself, "If I once let this envelope drop into the mailbox, this thing could snowball and I could end up being a single missionary in Panama—single for life!" But I took a deep breath, then let it drop!

"SET FOR THE DEFENSE OF THE GOSPEL"

THIS IS TO CERTIFY, that after a satisfactory relation
of his (or her) Christian experience, call to missionary
service, and views of Bible Doctrine,

MISS JEAN LITTLE

was this day, in behalf of the

Gospel Missionary Union
(INCORPORATED)

COMMISSIONED as a Missionary, fully authorized to ad-
minister all the ordinances of the Holy Scriptures.

Done this _20_ Day of _January_ in the Year of Our Lord _1955_

At _Kansas City_ , _Missouri_

Don Skeels
President

C. Kemmer

Stan Van Eygen

L. C. Weiss

Certificate of Appointment as a Career Missionary with the GMU.

Commencement of a Cross-Cultural Ministry

God's Appointment: Gospel Missionary Union

IN SEPTEMBER OF 1954, FELLOW BRIERCREST COLLEGE GRADUATES EARL AND SELMA, Ben and Adina and I traveled to Kansas City, Missouri, to attend Missionary Candidate School and Orientation. We found our way to the GMU headquarters at 1841 East 7th Street and settled in on the second floor of the GMU headquarters where we would spend the next five months.

Mrs. Shidler, wife of the President, directed the orientation program. A delightful lady with an eye for fashion and a gift for administration, she planned and arranged for language classes and tutors, assigned physical weekly duties and made sure we all knew etiquette and had good manners. Mrs. Shidler appointed us to various ministries in and around the city and placed each of us in situations where we would learn flexibility and adaptability.

The GMU headquarters also served as a retirement center for many missionaries. What an awesome honor to become acquainted with those who had served a lifetime in places like Ecuador, Morocco and the Mali Republic, West Africa! It was a unique privilege to be introduced to pioneer missionaries like George Reed, Maude Carey and Julia Anderson Woodward. I was awed by their selfless commitment to the calling of God to be instrumental in taking the Gospel to far-flung countries and peoples of the world.

Mrs. Woodward, who had spent fifty years in the highlands of Ecuador among the Quechua people, would be my Spanish language teacher. It was not unusual to begin a class eating papaya, avocado or a mango as she introduced me to tropical fruit that would soon be part of my diet. Mrs. Woodward was patient when, on occasion, I was certain that I had conjugated a verb correctly, only to be reminded that I was conjugating in French, not Spanish! Julia Woodward was truly blessed as a missionary, but most of her blessings came as subtractions rather than additions. When she flew to the States after fifty years in Ecuador, she knew of little fruit, yet praised God. For me personally, as a potential cross-cultural missionary, Julia Woodward became a role model like none other.

With five months of orientation completed, interviews with the GMU Board of Directors determined our direction. Somehow, we perceived them more as interrogations! Would we or would we not be appointed as career missionaries? The board members were godly men who asked tough questions, making the interviews intriguing experiences for each of us.

Following my interview I waited just like each one before me. The moment came when Dr. Shidler informed me that I was officially approved. He then added, "I was so afraid that one of the board members would ask you for your age!" Later, he confided, "When I went back into the board room, Dr. G. Christian Weiss asked, 'By the way, how old is that girl?'"

That is how it happened that, at twenty years of age, I became the youngest missionary to be accepted by the Gospel Missionary Union. I was appointed and licensed on January 26, 1955, for career missions in the country of Panama!

We left the next day for home. Earl, Selma and I were in Earl's new pick-up truck, while Ben and Adina followed in their older car. Earl tried to keep a close eye on them but lost track of them about three hours out of Kansas City. Turning around, he found Ben and Adina with a car whose engine was in big trouble and a pocketbook with insufficient funds for repairs.

Earl had thrown a long rope into the truck and now decided to use it to pull Ben and his car over one thousand kilometers back to Saskatchewan. The winter weather was incredibly cold and Ben had no heater in his car. As we drove, the rope kept breaking and what began as a thirty-foot rope was only six feet long by the time we reached home. I guess we believed that we were practicing the lessons of adaptability and flexibility learned at Candidate School! "Our Mrs. Shidler" had a different take. When hearing of our trip home, she commented, "Only the young and the foolish would do that!"

My twin sister remembers the terrible gut feeling of loneliness that she experienced when she learned of my appointment as a foreign missionary. She recalls how my dad was okay with my decision but, filled with emotion, asked, "But why does she have to go so far away?"

Deputation: Trusting God for Prayer and Financial Partners

As a twenty-one-year-old newly appointed missionary, I had no idea where to begin. Belonging to a faith mission meant trusting God for all my finances. I was also aware that I could not leave for Panama until one hundred percent of my financial support had been promised.

Deputation was a time of completely trusting God for financial support. There was no doubt in my heart that God had called, chosen and set me apart for cross-cultural ministry. Missionaries are "sent ones," so a partnership with a Team of Senders was necessary. It was definitely a new walk of faith, trusting God to direct my steps to those who would be part of the team.

I vividly recall how inadequate I felt as I began to write letters requesting the opportunity to speak in churches presenting the need of Panama. Who would even want someone without missionary experience, much less credibility, to speak in their churches? I cried out, "Where do I begin?"

Just where does one begin? Well, God is the best and only place to start.

I prayed. God brought to mind the name of Rev. Lloyd McDougall, a former beloved professor and now a pastor in the most southeastern part of Saskatchewan. I corresponded with him and he responded with grace, having arranged several opportunities for me to speak. I was overwhelmed with the generous hospitality offered by Rev. McDougall and his wife.

The day came when I would travel by bus to Estevan and the tour of churches would begin. After arriving in Estevan, it began to rain—and rain it did!—without stopping. The flood that resulted was not only devastating for everyone in the area but also for me personally. All my scheduled meetings were cancelled. I was incredibly discouraged. How do I start over? How do I begin again to find churches that would respond to my requests to share the calling of God on my life?

Sunday had come and gone and Monday had arrived. Where next and what now?

Pastor McDougall suggested that he call a friend in North Dakota who lived just a few miles across the border. He commented, "Perhaps he will give you an opportunity to share." He made the phone call. He offered to drive me to Cavalier, North Dakota, the next day.

As we traveled, I asked for details such as the pastor's name, the denomination of the church and other related questions. Pastor McDougall replied, "Oh, there is no church. There is no pastor and no denomination." His friend in North Dakota was a fairly new Christian and a car salesman. Pastor McDougall enthusiastically added, "But they have a Bible study in their small mobile trailer." My heart sank. No pastor! No church! New believers!

That Tuesday night, I shared my heart and my desire to serve in Panama with just a few in the living room of that small mobile home. I did not mention my financial need. I had just met "strangers" who took me in. The following morning my hosts, Wally and Gen, said that they would like to support me at seven dollars a month. I was elated!

Somehow, these new friends were not satisfied with just seven dollars. Wally told God, "If you provide more car sales, I will give more missionary support." Well, God took him up on his offer. That was the beginning of a twenty-year partnership with Wally and Gen. They did not miss a month! They were very generous in both financial and prayer support. My plan had been to find a church. God's plan was to find a Car Salesman with a missionary heart!

I was growing in amazement of who God is! He had just canceled several church appointments to bless me His way. He used Wally and Gen and, consequently, a wonderful church in Cavalier, North

Dakota, to provide far above and beyond my wildest expectations. I learned that when God sends a flood in Canada, He leads to dry land in the USA.

During one of several months of deputation, it was decided that Evelyn Stenbach, a missionary appointee to Morocco, and I would travel together. On one occasion we were scheduled to speak in a church in northern Saskatchewan. Upon our arrival in the early morning, we were met at the bus depot, with one whole day with our billet before the evening service. Our hostess was well prepared and had a plan!

This determined woman had yards of Pricilla frilly curtains that needed to be washed and ironed. Surely two missionaries could get them all ironed and back up before nightfall. Evie and I will never forget that day—two irons and two ironing boards and yards of curtains. Guess she wanted to know of what kind of stuff we were made.

Evie was a Scandinavian who loved her black coffee. I enjoyed my coffee with cream and sugar. I was very shy and did not have the courage to ask for whatever was not on the table, so I never asked for cream and sugar. I thought to myself, "I will drink this coffee black if it kills me!" Well, I've been drinking black coffee ever since.

Later, the renowned People's Church of Toronto extended an invitation to be one of their many missionaries. For twenty years they faithfully and generously provided both financial and prayer support. It was a privilege to host both Dr. Oswald Smith and his son Dr. Paul Smith in our home when they visited Panama at different times.

Eight months of travel provided fascinating experiences and many memories of God's wonderful provision. He brought into my life those who would serve as prayer and financial partners. One young woman in South Dakota gave two dollars a month for twenty years without missing a month. During one furlough, I visited her and was so humbled to see her small sparsely furnished apartment. She had so little but joyfully shared out of her poverty.

Other friends who were themselves engaged in Christian ministry contributed from their limited budgets. One couple had endured financial hardship on their first overseas assignment. They returned to their Canadian home with only $57.00 in their pockets. Out of their poverty they prayed and gave. They never missed a month. I was so blessed with friends with missionary hearts and so humbled and grateful to be part of their team.

Hudson Taylor, founder of China Inland Mission, had a policy that he would never make known his financial needs to anyone. He believed that if God knew what he needed, why tell anyone else? I also adopted his plan and, like Hudson Taylor, I saw God provide. It was enough just to tell Him.

Which is Harder: To Leave or to be Left Behind?

Nine months after my appointment it was time to leave for my five-year term in Panama. I calculated and thought, "I am single. I am twenty-one. I am probably the most uninformed person that ever landed on a mission field." I had not taken courses in anthropology, church planting or cross-cultural communication. In reality, I had limited orientation and preparation for missionary work. I was fearful yet confident that this was the calling of God on my life.

The memory of my departure is indelible and bittersweet. I was to travel by train from Moose Jaw, Saskatchewan, to Winnipeg, Manitoba. I would then fly to Panama City via Kansas City. Bidding farewell was going to be tough. Staying in Kansas City for a couple of weeks was of little comfort. I might as well have been on another continent as far as any contact with family.

The day arrived. I didn't want to cry. I knew that my mom, being very emotional, would cry. I would be strong and not shed a tear, even though I knew that final moments for families can be devastating. Mom wept as we embraced for a long time. Then, as I hugged my dad, I totally lost it! As I boarded the train I began to sob and could not stop. I believed that my dad, at age sixty-six, was elderly and I would not see him again. I can't remember just how long the tears fell. The hole and pain in my heart were unbearable. I felt very much alone. I cried out to the Lord. In those moments, He reminded me that the promise of His presence was a reality—I AM with you always. The promise to make disciples of all nations was always accompanied by the reality of His presence.

At this time in mission history, a missionary term was long and uninterrupted. The thought of coming home before the completion of a term was unthinkable. There was no such thing as a short-term mentality. Skype, text messaging and emails were nonexistent. I would not hear the voices of my parents or my siblings for five years.

I realized then that, even in obedience, there is pain and hurt. Today, I ask myself the questions: Which is harder, to leave or to be left behind? Both are painful. In my youthful self-preoccupation, I thought only of my own pain of separation. I failed to envision the tears of my family, who could barely endure a five-year wait. Now, years later, I also understand the implications of leaving and being left behind, as I have bid farewell to my adult children on more than one occasion at more than one airport.

Goodbyes at airports are never easy, and somehow, they never get easier. There is pain in obedience—Jesus knew it well. Max Lucado eloquently described it as he penned, "Leaving is Loving."

It seems that goodbye is a word all too prevalent in the Christian's vocabulary. Missionaries know it well. Those who send them know it, too. The doctor who leaves the city to work in the jungle hospital has said it. So has the Bible translator who lives far from home. Those who feed the hungry those who teach the lost,

Those who help the poor all know the word goodbye.

Airports. Luggage. Embraces. Taillights. "Wave to Grandma" Tears.Bus terminals. Ship docks. "Goodbye Daddy," Tight throats. Ticket-counters. Misty eyes. "Write me!"

Question: What kind of God would put people through such agony? What kind of God would give you families and then ask you to leave them? What kind of God would give you friends and then ask you to say goodbye?

Answer: A God who knows that the deepest love is built not on passion and romance but on a common mission and sacrifice.

Answer: A God who knows that we are only pilgrims and that eternity is so close that any "Goodbye" is in reality a "See you tomorrow." Answer: A God who did it Himself.[4]

In those final moments, God understood.

Panama, the Next Step: Preparation for Departure

My first term was to include a year of language study at the Language Institute in San Jose, Costa Rica. With passport and visa in hand just before my departure, I was notified that I would bypass Costa Rica and go directly to Panama following a short time at our mission headquarters in Kansas City.

My two weeks at the Kansas City headquarters left little room for concern or curiosity about this extraordinary shift in plans. Most days were committed to shopping and packing missionary barrels.

On the eve of the missionary's departure, it was tradition that those living at the Mission Home would gather in the chapel. It was to be a time of blessing the "outgoing missionary" with promises from God's Word. It was a marvelous oasis, one I will never forget.

One after the other, staff, candidates, appointees, furloughing missionaries and visitors arose to their feet, giving me promises from the Word. There were many verses that focused on God's presence, peace and faithfulness.

Of all the promises given, there is only one verse that I remember. Retired missionary Julia Woodward stood and gave me Hebrews 12:15, "Let no root of bitterness spring up and cause trouble, and by this many will become defiled." At the time I puzzled, "What a curious promise!" Now, fifty seven years later, it is the one and only still engraved on my mind.

---

[4] Max Lucado, *No Wonder They Call Him The Savior* (Portland, OR: Multnomah Press, 1986), 20.

Realities of a First Missionary Term

On Location in Panama: Language Learning

I ARRIVED ON BRANIFF AIRLINES ON A SATURDAY NIGHT, OCTOBER 22, 1955. DEL AND Noreen Reimer met me at the Panama Tocumen Airport. They invited me to stay with them the first few days in their home at the GMU Center, located on a ten acre farm with every fruit imaginable, elegant palm trees lining the driveway and breathtaking bougainvillea. The first missionaries named it "El Amanecer," or in English, "Sunrise Farm." Down through the years, it became just "the Farm." The clarity of that first night is still vivid with all its sensory color. I heard, for the first time, rhythmic Latin voices, melodic laughter, lively dance music and the reverberating drums from the "cantina" pub across the street. I had arrived.

Two years earlier, Linda Reimer, a registered nurse and twenty years my senior, became the first GMU missionary to arrive in Panama. Linda had served several years in Puerto Rico, arriving in Panama with fluent Spanish. Linda would be my first Spanish language instructor. Later, other classes would be added in the nearby city of La Chorrera, with Panamanian professors.

On Monday morning the plan was to join other recently arrived missionaries for language classes. Eighteen of us had arrived within twelve months.

I soon discovered the real reason for bypassing Language School in Costa Rica. Three single young women from the Mission had been somewhat distracted in their studies. Possible change of marital status threatened their intended postings. The Mission decided not to risk another potential casualty. So I flew over, rather than land in Costa Rica, and went directly to "the Farm" in Panama. Really, I did not think of myself as any kind of risk!

Following the same schedule begun as a college student, I developed a plan for focused language learning. Self-motivation became a reality as I arose each morning at six, followed by devotions and breakfast, just as I had done at school. One-hour blocks of reading, conjugating verbs, new vocabulary, reading and assignments became the routine of each weekday.

From the very beginning, I also worked out a game plan for Sundays. The pastor's sermon proved to be a great context for learning. I devised a program of first learning words then understanding the sermon topic, followed by an attempt to understand the outline. It would have been easier to daydream and permit my mind to wander in a hundred different directions, but I did not allow myself that luxury.

On the first day of Spanish classes, I learned that one of my assignments would be to cross the highway and spend a half hour each day in a Panamanian hut, practicing conversational Spanish. Well, I had just arrived—not even forty-eight hours earlier—having bypassed language school! Surely this assignment would not include me. I didn't have any idea how to form Spanish sentences, so I asked, "Am I also expected to do this?"

Linda's answer was a resounding "Yes. My coworker Helen will soon be here to take you across the highway." Helen arrived as promised. I went, not yet adjusted, but expected to go!

Four years of high school French was not any preparation for that half hour! As days passed I got weary of repeating the few words and brief sentences I knew. I had a quiet moment of rebellion in my heart at the tedious repetition. I was getting tired of asking the names of the children, the names of the dogs, the number of chickens. I had exhausted my vocabulary. The day came when I tried to graciously tell my teacher to mark me absent from this assignment for the following day. I did not want to cross the highway and I could not face another half hour of conversational Spanish with my limited vocabulary.

The next morning, my Spanish class was dismissed, and within an hour, I saw Leander and his son Regino coming down the hill to my home. Linda had crossed the highway, requesting they spend two hours with me. They were not to leave before two hours was up! Two hours trying to listen and understand was much more difficult than a half-hour conversation! Well, the next day, with due resignation, I crossed the highway without objection. I can't thank the Lord enough for Linda, a great and persevering Spanish language instructor! I soon understood that one can learn words from a textbook, but one can only learn a language from people.

Which language I should use for my personal Bible study? Spanish or English? Spanish was my first inclination, but saturating myself in my well-used English Bible was imperative. Personal Bible study and devotional times in English were necessary so when I would be fluent in the language, I could share His Word from the overflow of my heart.

A two-year language study program had been designed for those of us who were learning Spanish on location. I was focused, determined and dedicated. This focus and determination inspired a goal. I had a competitive heart and I secretly targeted to compete with one missionary. My goal was to finish and the complete the course in less than two years and before he did. Who won? Well, I think we finished about the same time!

Experiencing God's Provision

These first months on the Sunrise Farm were idyllic. This ten-acre fruit farm had been bought by the mission. Its long, graceful entrance was lined with palm trees with white washed bottoms. There were orange and grapefruit trees, bananas galore, pineapple, passion fruit and much more, all for the taking.

Several houses inhabited the property. Families who had recently arrived lived in a couple of homes near the entrance of the Farm. Two single women lived in a delightful little house in the middle of the property. My humble cement home was at the far end of the property and on the edge of the gully. Many days were occupied with language learning, which was thoroughly enjoyable, though tough. It was at night that loneliness set in.

Evenings in Panama are beautiful and warm. Each night after supper and dishes were done, I would take a walk. Across the clear night sky I could hear laughter, chatting and busy family banter. From time to time passing by screen windows, I could hear evening devotions and prayers. Discerning little and large voices as I sauntered paths simply reinforced and confirmed my loneliness. Loneliness did not dominate my life, but neither was it entirely absent. I remember writing to my mom and dad on the evening of November 22, 1955. I lamented, "I have been here for exactly one month. In four years and eleven months, I get to come home!"

We used coal oil lamps and kerosene fridges and stoves. There was no running water and every function was incredibly simplistic. However, this didn't bother me in the least, as I had been raised on a farm without a whole lot of conveniences. I just thought this was the way missionary life was meant to be.

It had only been a few weeks since my arrival on the field and promised financial support had not yet been sent to the mission office. In my wallet I had one quarter—only twenty-five cents! A decision must be made. Would I spend the twenty-five cents on batteries for my one and only flashlight? That flashlight was unbelievably important, as darkness covered the farm shortly after supper time. The bathroom was down the path on the edge of the gully where snakes slithered in the leaves. I also needed food. My cupboards were bare. There was little to eat. So, was it food or batteries? I had a decision to make. I bought the batteries.

Later in the afternoon I crossed the highway to practice my Spanish. As I entered a small village, I met a little wrinkled elderly Panamanian woman. She had been waiting for me. Her smile was contagious. She held up a bunch of small apple bananas. She exclaimed, "I picked these bananas just for you. I was hoping that you would come." I was amazed! God beautifully blessed me by this simple act of kindness from one who had so very little herself. It was no mistake that on this particular afternoon a single twenty-one-year-old missionary far from Mom but near to God would learn of His provision. He who called also cared. God said that He would provide. He kept His promise.

Our First Assignment

After more than four months of living alone in the small house at the back of the property on the edge of the gully, I learned that another single young woman was soon to arrive in Panama.

Ruth Schjeveland was a third generation American Canal Zone resident, her grandfather having arrived in Panama many years earlier to work on the construction of the Panama Canal. After becoming a Christian, Ruth attended and graduated from Moody Bible Institute in Chicago. We met for the first time in Kansas City at the GMU headquarters, where we both were part of the mission's orientation program.

During that specific time in Panama no one thought of personalities, preferences or personal choices. Whoever was the next to arrive was just automatically placed with the previous newcomer. Three single missionary women arrived that year. Interestingly enough, each of us had a twin sister! Mary had a Martha, Dorothy had a Doris, and Jean had a Joan. Ruth arrived in February the following year, and since I was the last to arrive, we were assigned to live together.

Then one day, without our knowledge, it was decided that Ruth and I would move to Campana, a small town in the interior at the foot of the mountain. Our house was chosen and rented for us and we were given our church planting appointment. Neither Ruth nor I were part of the discussion; the decision was made and confirmed before we were aware of what was happening. Unlike a generation that desires to participate in the decision-making process, we did not think it strange or even question the procedure.

In the early part of 1956, we moved to the village of Campana. We settled into a small cement house with a colored stone front porch, a zinc roof, screen doors and windows and one dividing wall that did not reach the ceiling. The bathroom was a small shack at the end of the path behind the house. It was amazing how soon one could become accustomed to taking bucket showers. However, the realization that the neighbors knew our daily bath time routine was a more difficult adjustment.

Ruth and I become very close friends, although it was not always this way. It took many discussions and several disagreements, but we made a decision. We had five years ahead of us. Our differences must not hinder our desire to share the Gospel. We couldn't allow any bitterness to spring up and take root. In the process of time we learned to laugh together, pray together and enjoy ministry together.

We were total opposites in every way. She was a night person and I preferred to get up early in the morning. The only dividing wall in our house didn't go to the top and curtains hung where doors were meant to be—there was not a whole lot of privacy. Our ministry strategies were philosophically miles apart. We disagreed about how to start a church from scratch.

I have forgotten many details of those early years, but I do remember very clearly the first day Ruth was cooking. It was my week for cleaning duty, so I relinquished the kitchen. Ruth prepared scrambled eggs for breakfast. Though Ruth's lunch main dish for that day is forgotten, her dessert is not. "Ruth," I asked, "what are all these black spots in the vanilla pudding?"

She blithely replied, "Oh, that is the pepper in the leftover scrabbled eggs from breakfast. They mixed nicely with the pudding."

Recipe books became essential in the kitchen. We both needed to both grow in our culinary skills.

Our finances were not ample, so we bought some chicks and asked Mino, a new believer to raise them for us, which he did. Each time roast chicken was on the dinner menu, we would trek down the street and ask Mino to kill and clean a chicken. Everyone in the whole village knew when Ruth and I were having a chicken dinner. Then the day came when I decided that this was enough—I would do it myself. I had often watched my mom "clean" chickens. I was sure I could pluck it, gut it and clean it! I did. I remembered exactly what my mom had done. She had taught me well as she informally mentored me while I was sitting on a stool in the farm kitchen.

We were thankful for this delightful town with one main street lined on both sides by mud huts with thatched roofs. As we settled in, we continued with a two-year Spanish study. Again we were reminded that one can learn words from books, but one learns a language from people.

Language learning is a lifetime experience. The completion of the two-year Spanish course did not mean that I was finished learning. I looked for ways to continue, so I began to seek someone who would teach me the idiomatic phrases that were unique only to Panama. A new believer approached his sister about the possibility. Edna, an elementary school teacher, agreed to teach me. We had an hour around her dining room table each week. Today, nearly sixty years later and separated by thousands of miles, Edna and I enjoy a close friendship.

We were settled and eager, and we had learned some Spanish, but just where does one begin to plant a church when one doesn't have a Church Planting Manual? Relationships were obviously key, but it takes time to build friendships and trust.

We wanted to engage with our community. We certainly felt insufficient for the task before us, but God had equipped us with gifts and we believed doors would open. Ruth loved children and they loved her. Little ones would begin the day by planting their noses against our screen windows and watching our every move. Privacy had become a thing of the past. In reality, we were a perplexity. They were convinced that we were deaf because whenever we could not understand a Spanish word or phrase, we would often ask, "What did you say?" They would then simply repeat their words as quickly as before, but very much louder! Off they would go again! The children never gave up on us.

No amount of casual conversation could unravel the reluctance we were occasionally met with. We were curious and puzzled. Much later, we discovered that a few town folk believed we must be lesbians. Two women just did not live together unless they were practicing that lifestyle. So, they assumed and concluded that we were two deaf American lesbian women who had come to live among them. Thankfully, God can unravel misperceptions.

Singleness

Singleness, the very thing that I feared the most, became the platform for immersion into both language and culture. It takes time, much time, to learn a new language and transition into another culture. I thank God for the privilege of singleness that allowed me to dedicate as much time as needed for language acquisition and culture immersion.

Vacations can be problematic for singles in different parts of the world, but that was not our case. There were six, and at times eight, single women on the field, so vacations alone were never an issue. One of our favorite vacation spots was Santa Clara in Panama's interior.

Four single women on our first vacation together will not easily be forgotten! Mary, Dorothy, Ruth and I rented a lovely cottage on the shores of the Pacific Ocean, where walking the sandy beaches early in the morning or on moonlit nights became a favorite pastime.

On our first evening we decided to play a game of Monopoly. However, we had no idea that there would be such stiff competition among us. Buying and selling hotels and properties on the Monopoly board became an issue. One of us would not sell one of her hotels and ... well, the rest is history. Needless to say, we stopped playing Monopoly during the vacation, but we have never stopped being friends.

Of course, singleness is not all fun and games. It definitely has its struggles, mostly associated with loneliness and misunderstandings. Singleness also gives opportunity for concerned and loving friends to both encourage and discourage relationships. It all made for interesting days!

Singleness provided special opportunities to spend time with those who were part of our missionary family. It was fun to be called "Auntie" by many missionary kids, to whom now, years later, I am still "Aunt Jean." Each Tuesday evening we met in the home of Aaron and Imageyne for Bible study and prayer, followed by chocolate cake and ice cream. Their kids seemed like our own. It is interesting that, after more than fifty years, we still consider one another "family."

Culture Shock

Campana boasted of one long lonely street. At one end was a water pump and at the other, the Post Office. Ruth and I daily debated who would take the trek down the main street. Neither of us wanted to. Mingling with the neighborhood was essential, but some neighborhood habits were irritating, such as a few idle men sitting on their haunches staring at us as we walked down the only street.

We had no idea that what we were going through was culture shock! We did not know that culture shock has both symptoms and stages. I know now, but I didn't know then. The symptoms are negativism and isolation. Ruth and I were experiencing both but did not know it.

Today, years later, I understand that the stages of culture shock involve four elements: fascination, frustration, funny and failure. I had gone through the fascination stage. During my first year in Panama's interior, I was fascinated seeing some women use a wringer washing machine to roll out the dough for tortillas. Some new believers carried their tithe in their ears! I was fascinated by the fact that a women would go to court to determine which rock by the river was her possession while washing clothes. I was fascinated by superstitious beliefs practiced decades ago, such as if one would climb a tree on Good Friday, one would turn into a monkey . . . and on and on.

I was intrigued by their community spirit. On a lonely afternoon as I neared Campana, the big Chrysler I was driving had a flat tire. As I was viewing my situation, a Panamanian bus called a "chiva" drove up and stopped. The driver told all the passengers to get off the bus and help. Their knowledge of car jacks was limited, but that did not deter them. In one accord they lifted the car, fixed the tire and on count returned the car to its position. Then, one by one, the village "Good Samaritans" boarded the bus and a new missionary from Canada drove home in total disbelief.

I enjoyed this stage. However, it does end. Years later, I found myself telling my "would-be-missionary-students" to take all their pictures in the fascination stage because after that things become mundane and ordinary. When I think of it, it doesn't take long for the strange to become normal!

After the fascination, frustration sets in. I was stymied by inability to express. Though I was studying, I could not properly communicate ideas and thoughts. The words I needed were not yet part of my vocabulary. Because I was determined, focused and positive, I did not spend much time in this stage. For many, without help and proper understanding, frustration can cripple. But God understands culture shock. Through missions history, even before culture shock was labeled, God enabled adjustment for those He called.

A welcome reprieve after the frustration is the funny stage. It is at this stage we can laugh at our own cultural and language blunders. It took me a while to learn how to laugh at myself and not take life so seriously. Thank God, I never got to the final stage, failure. It is a grievous loss when a missionary exits the field when failing to adjust.

We had no idea of the symptoms and stages of culture shock. If only someone would have explained it all to us! I doubt if the early pioneer missionaries such as the Moravians, William Carey or Hudson Taylor ever had a lesson in culture shock either! God undergirded and intervened to give victory.

Evangelism and Discipleship: The Beginning of a Church

Upon arriving in Campana, of course, neither my coworker nor I were fluent in the Spanish language. We didn't let that stop us. A smile, a bit of sign language, a few words to inspire laughter . . . it was enough to lay a foundation. Even when we saw grief and pain, we did not hesitate. We could express our love and care. We just needed to be there. We really did not need to say a thing. An embrace and our presence was enough. We were reminded of Jesus, whose purpose for His incarnation was foretold by the prophet Isaiah, *"He has sent Me to heal the brokenhearted, to proclaim liberty to the captives, and the opening of the prison to those who are bound . . . to console those who mourn in Zion, to give them beauty for ashes, the oil of joy for mourning, the garment of praise for the spirit of heaviness"* (Isaiah 61:1–3, NKJV).

Not long after we had settled into our little cement home, we met neighbors down the street. We learned that a young couple's newly born baby had unexpectedly died. That evening the wake began. In the center of the living room stood the tiny open casket. Family, friends and neighbors gathered. They said nothing, but circling the baby, wept with the parents. We joined them, took the chairs offered and remained all night. We didn't understand everything as all was new to us. Our prayer that night was that in some way our presence would express the love of Jesus, the One who came to heal the brokenhearted.

As time went on young people began to stop by. We would spend hours visiting on our long porch. Later we invited them to join us in studying the Bible. They started to come, the numbers grew and the porch became too small. What to do now?

In Campana, two beer parlors (called "cantinas") were located on the same side of the street just blocks from each other. One was called "Aqui me quedo" (Here I remain!). The other was for sale. We bought it. The bar top was removed and it became the sidewalk to the front door. That small cantina transformed into our first church. God began to draw those whose hearts He had prepared, and one after another, young adults and teenagers came to faith in Christ.

Life in Campana at the outset was not without opposition. There were those who attempted to disturb our meetings and to remind us that we were not wanted. Others sought ways to get us out of town. There were a few who definitely did not hide their hatred for evangelicals. Building confidence and relationships was a slow process and there definitely were days of discouragement, but we were where God had placed us.

Life in a small village was at times challenging, sometimes lonely and often tiring, but we understood that we were in Panama's interior by God's appointment. The slower pace of the villages provided opportunities for discipleship, where hours were spent teaching and leading Bible studies. Young men and women were soon giving leadership in the church, leading in devotions, teaching Sunday school and conducting choirs.

Within time, we discovered that the chief export of rural Panama is not bananas but young people. Several who trusted Christ demonstrated new purpose and focus for their futures. Many were drawn away, looking to further their education, get employment and begin careers. It was a continual challenge to establish a church when new Christians, balancing purpose and survival, left for the city.

The small village of Campana has given to the world key Christian leaders who, decades ago as teenagers, yielded their lives to God. Among them are university professors, pastors, hospital administrators and Christian leaders. Many of their children and grandchildren are faithfully following the Lord, with some becoming global workers.

Member Care

Six decades ago "member care" wasn't even a distant thought, much less assumed or expected, but it was definitely experienced. Illustrations of God's member care through others was abundant.

My dear mom wrote every Sunday for twenty years. There was not even one week without a newsy letter from her. I was well aware that she wrote those letters at night after extending hospitality to guests and blessing many during afternoon hospital visitations. I know she must have been weary and it would have been easier to go to bed rather than begin a letter. Mom was so faithful and I was so blessed. Dad's love was equally appreciated as he expressed his devotion through financial support, not missing a month for nearly twenty years. That was member care.

Every letter and parcel was anticipated. How we loved to receive news from family and friends. I recall specific letters from friends who wrote just like they spoke, always putting a smile on my face. Each time we walked down that long street to the post office, despite the ever-present onlookers, we walked with anticipation. Sometimes there were only letters, but on occasion, we were surprised by care packages. It is difficult to put into words the delight at receiving that brown packaged box plastered with stamps from North America. Many of the gifts received had been opened with items removed. We were unsure of what they took. However, we were grateful for what they left. That was member care!

On more than one occasion I would receive a letter which was significant. They were letters I will never forget. Well, they weren't really letters, but coffee stained paper napkins tucked in an envelope with a personal handwritten address. In a corner of the napkin in a space with no coffee stains were these words, "I prayed for you today, Phil. 1:6." He simply signed his name, Don P. Shidler. There were no added designations such as President or C.E.O. That was member care!

Frequently, Ruth would receive a handwritten letter from her pastor, Dr. Alan Redpath, Senior Pastor of the Moody Church in Chicago. That was member care!

As I sit and think about all the member care I received, more stories come to mind than space to record them. Loving care is a biblical principle. Loving, encouraging and ministering to one another is what we do. Many do it so well. I will never cease to be in awe of the significance of belonging to the family of God.

Surprises of a Canadian Home Service

Returning to Canada

FIVE YEARS HAD PASSED. GMU MISSION POLICY REQUIRED FIVE YEARS ON THE FIELD followed by one year at home. It was called "furlough" and there were few exceptions.

The village of Campana had become "home." Leaving would be tough. Everyone in town knew our departure date was getting closer and a year away would soon be a reality. They responded with their hearts and we were overwhelmed with their gracious gifts. Many gifts were handcrafted by our neighbors and we were recipients of their loving generosity.

However, there were those who were not giving, but getting what they could! It happened just a week before our departure. Ruth had left to spend a few days on the Atlantic side of the Isthmus, while I remained in town for the weekend.

On that particular weekend, several of the young people came to the house for games and fellowship on Saturday evening. I thought they would never go home. So I had an idea. I suggested to Elisa, "Why don't you cross the street to your house, get what you need and come back to spend the night with me?" She loved the idea.

That particular night the rain poured heavily down on our tin roof. It was deafening. Elisa prepared the sofa in the living room where she would sleep. I went to my bedroom. I awoke startled in the middle of the night. I sat up, only to discover a man on my bed! I opened my mouth to scream, but nothing came out. What a terrible sensation! It gave me a new understanding of the cliché "scared to death!"

As I sat up, the intruder retreated and climbed out of the window. I waited until he was out before I awoke my dear friend on the living room sofa. Using our flashlights, we investigated, and there was plenty of evidence. While the deafening rain pounded down on our zinc roof, two men cut the screens in my bedroom window, climbed inside and onto my bed, continuing to light their way into the house by using matches. It was unbelievable that the bed sheets did not catch on fire!

We later discovered that one of the two men had just been released from jail. Both men believed that I was alone. They assumed that I must have enough money in the house to make the trip to Canada. They decided they needed that money more than I did.

God's protection and provision were amazing! He had beautifully orchestrated the events of the previous evening in such a way that my neighbor Elisa was with me. The next morning she became the Town Crier, pacing the street proclaiming, "I am sleeping with my machete under my pillow tonight. If someone tries to get into Juanita's house tonight, beware!

As I was ready to leave Campana, there were missionaries who asked me to phone certain family members and give them personal greetings. I agreed to make the phone calls and deliver the messages. Cliff and Diana Reimer mentioned, "Should you ever happen to be near Steinbach, Manitoba, say hello to our families." I agreed to do my best.

Flight plans were made, tickets were bought, suitcases packed and it was time to head for the airport. Several of my dearest Panamanian friends were at the airport to bid me farewell. Saying, "goodbye" was tough and didn't come easy!

Ruth and I left Panama on different days of the same week. Ruth did not return to Panama but took a position at Moody Church in the Spanish department. It was a very sad day when, years later, I learned that Ruth had unexpectedly passed away. Ruth left a lasting legacy of her love for Jesus and for children.

After a long flight, several stops and one train ride, I was home! My twin sister took her two-week vacation to be home when I arrived. As wonderful as it all was, I found myself uneasy. It had never dawned on me that I would be jarred by the change, that differences would be so significant. Incredibly lonesome for those I had left behind, I resisted adjustments required of me. I was overwhelmed. I wanted to be alone! I had no idea that I was going through reverse culture shock. From my family's perspective, I had come home. From mine, I had left home. I had left my heart in Panama and my gut ached.

Beth Maxfield Ashabraner describes it well:

> "I am a child of the world. I am at ease in distant lands and yet my spirit feels strangely out of place at home."[5]

However, it was exciting to be back in the kitchen where I grew up surrounded by family. They were such an inspiration, surprising me with inquiries regarding our believers as they mentioned each one by name. Their questions were prompted by five years "on their knees" praying specifically for our church in Campana. One of my parents' greatest rewards was the visit of one of the believers who, with his wife and family, drove many miles to personally express their gratitude for years of intercession for them.

I loved my church family and was grateful for the overwhelming embrace extended me. My "Welcome Home" dinner remains a treasured memory. I walked into the basement of the church, where tables were set for a lovely meal and Russian thistle and tumbleweed were stapled to the walls. I loved their creativity! I was back in Saskatchewan!

Adjustment takes time but comes easier with the understanding and love of family and friends. I gratefully reoriented myself to their community and care. There was little time to mope, what with the demands of my schedule. It was a special time designed to personally thank those who had faithfully prayed and given, many of them sacrificially. A term of missionary service in Panama would not have happened without them.

---

[5] Bethany Maxfield, "A Savior's Scribbles." *Missions Publication of The Church of God* Vol.66 No 5 (September/October 2002).

Conferences and meetings were the order of the day and very much a part of a home assignment. One particular conference would have special significance. Mardelle, a fellow GMU missionary, joined me as we attended a missions conference in southern Manitoba. Mardelle and I spent one entire night on our knees praying about God's direction in our lives. The prayer was timely. He knew we both would be meeting with a detour.

A Divine Appointment and Meeting

Throughout the missions conference, Danny, a missionary appointee and a close friend of Cliff's brother, repeatedly suggested that I meet his friend Gil. I didn't pay much attention . . . but I didn't forget, either!

At the conclusion of the conference, I received a phone call from Cliff's parents inviting me to spend the weekend in their home. I accepted their gracious invitation, as I did not have another appointment scheduled. It would be my joy to personally deliver the greetings from their children, Cliff and Diana, and granddaughters, Corinne and Heather.

During the phone call, it was decided that Cliff's brother Gil would pick me up at the Dodge dealership in Steinbach. Gil, a high school teacher in Glenboro, Manitoba, was home for the weekend. That Saturday morning was my first introduction to Gil Reimer. His mom was expecting him to bring home a middle-aged single missionary woman, perhaps with her hair in a bun, whose name was "Miss Little." When Mrs. Reimer greeted me at the front door, her mouth literally fell open. She had not anticipated a young woman in her twenties who didn't quite look like the missionary she had imagined.

It was a privilege to meet Cliff's parents Mr. and Mrs. Ben L. Reimer, brother Lawrence and younger sister Noreen. There was one more sister, Evangeline, whom I met later. I also had the joy of meeting Diana's parents, Mr. and Mrs. Henry Toews.

I recognized soon that Cliff's family were well informed about what God was doing in the world. Mr. Reimer, who had traveled extensively overseas with the Manitoba Marketing Board, was also very aware of the global scene. On his business trips he chose to stay at missionary guest houses rather than hotels. He believed these sojourns would give him greater insight into what God was doing around the world.

Global missions was very much a part of their ethos, with a special personal interest in Gospel Missionary Union. They had entertained President Dr. Don P. and Mrs. Shidler many times in their home whenever he ministered in the Steinbach area. They also had a personal interest, as their son and his family served as educators in the country of Panama. They also knew what it meant to say goodbye to children and grandchildren.

During that weekend visit our conversations were easy and intriguing. The Reimer family were exceptional hosts and made me feel very much at home. Who was this handsome young unattached Gil Reimer that I had just met? His sister Vange Doerksen gives insight into his early years . . .

Gil grew up on a farm in a loving Christian home. His father was an entrepreneur, always community minded, who served on several boards. Mom's gift was hospitality. Their home was always open to missionaries, friends, neighbors and anyone who needed a meal or a bed. We children were never privy to any fights between mom and dad—disagreements sometimes, but no harsh words. There was always mutual love and respect as they modeled a wonderful marriage.

From a very young age, Gil enjoyed reading and learning. Several times at age three, he would run away to school. On those days the teacher kept him in school until Dad would come to get him. Gil assumed that unless the teacher threw him out, he was welcome. Gil's thirst for knowledge was evident in the fact that he could read well before grade one. On his first day at school he was placed into grade two.

His increasing interest in music was evident in his ability to play the piano, mandolin and cello. He also taught himself to read notes and taught himself to sing in harmony. Gil was not easily overwhelmed by any task, becoming a leader to organize special family events. The story of the five missionaries martyred by the Woadani tribe had a significant affect on Gil. I remember gathering around the piano singing the martyrs' signature song, 'We Rest on Thee Our Shield and Our Defender.' This song touched his heart. Music has a way of doing this.

Shortly after meeting the Reimer family, I returned to my Saskatchewan farm home. I realized that, with winter just around the corner, opportunities to report on missions would be sparse. I needed God's clear direction for the few months ahead. After much prayer, God prompted me to apply to the Canadian office of Back to the Bible Broadcast in Winnipeg, and within a few days, I was offered a position. Dear friends offered me a temporary place to hang my hat until God provided a more permanent place.

Serving Jesus in the Back to the Bible office proved to be invigorating and the camaraderie and fellowship of the staff rewarding. After being blessed by the generous hospitality of Del and Noreen, I moved into an apartment on Portage Avenue with three young women. Great friendships developed and grew.

It was also during these winter months that Gil and I would end up attending some of the same functions in the city. I recall one occasion when I acted a little "snobbish," simply because I did not want anyone to assume a single missionary was trying to attract the attention of an eligible bachelor!

Then it happened. One evening the phone rang. The call could have been for any one of us four. The shock was not that the call was for me but that it was a call from Gil. He invited me to join him for dinner and later attend the symphony in Winnipeg. I accepted his kind invitation without even praying about it. For this special occasion, I recall choosing an appropriate dress with costume jewelry to match, only to discover much later that Gil disliked costume jewelry! Oh well, it didn't appear to alter his thinking or change his mind about another date!

During dinner at Gerry's Steak House on Portage Avenue that evening, I learned that he had two years of Bible school under his belt but continued as a high school teacher rather than return for a final year at Steinbach Bible Institute. Gil also described his process of presently making application to GMU to serve as a teacher in Latin America. I asked, "What is prompting you to leave the security of North American tenure?"

He told me, "While you were on furlough in Canada, I flew to Panama to spend Christmas vacation with my brother Cliff, sister-in-law Diana and my two nieces, Corinne and Heather. I immediately fell in love with the people and their country. Before returning to Canada, a young Panamanian man named Jorge asked me when I would be back to stay. His question was instrumental and prompted me to seek God's wisdom and direction towards missionary work, but it was not the first Holy Spirit prompting. A few years before, my heart was incredibly stirred by the story of the martyrdom of the five missionaries speared to death in Ecuador."

Before the end of the academic year, Gil resigned from Glenboro High School and prepared to return to the Steinbach Bible Institute to fulfill the Bible requirements of GMU.

Engaged to Be Married

Four months before my scheduled return to Panama and three months before the first class of Gil's final year at Steinbach Bible Institute, we were engaged.

Shortly after our engagement, we received word from our Kansas City headquarters suggesting that my furlough be extended for us to be married. However, at the same time a letter arrived from Panama asking that I return to Panama as previously planned. We were faced with a huge decision. The invitation to remain in Canada longer and get married sooner was very inviting. As we prayed and sought God, it became evidently clear that I should return to Panama for one more year, single, but with a diamond on my hand!

On the return flight to Panama my prayer was specific. I asked God to guard my tongue against unceasing talk about wedding plans so not to weary my coworkers with nuptial details. I asked for sensitivity for those who might not marry. Returning to Campana for that one year became one of my most notable years as a single woman. My coworker, Mary, and I were not only friends but confidantes and shared many prayer requests unknown to others. It was a year filled with the blessings of spiritual growth and exciting anticipation.

Our Wedding: One Year Later

The following year just six weeks before our wedding, I flew back to Canada. The date had been set for June 16, 1962. After spending time in Saskatchewan with my family, I returned to Manitoba. Life became a whirl-wind of activity and joyous planning. The wedding ceremony and reception would happen in Woodrow Gospel Chapel in Woodrow, Saskatchewan. This was my home church and I was overwhelmed with the love extended to me. Jehovah Jireh, my Provider, was evident at every juncture. I had little time to shuttle between obligations to two families, my church and endless wedding demands. My calendar with all the appointments was never out of my sight. I saw God take care of every detail.

While in Manitoba I would shop for my bridal gown in the city of Winnipeg. I was happy and sad all at the same time, knowing my mom would not share this special day with me. I truly treasured her advice and companionship. Alone, I tramped the downtown streets of Winnipeg from one bridal store to the next. At the end of the day my feet ached—I was exhausted but successful. I had found the wedding gown. It was conservative and classic and I made plans to return the following day to buy it. Contentment filled my heart.

Then everything changed.

While attending a surprise bridal shower that evening, one of Gil's cousins offered to lend me her wedding dress. Unbelievable! Appreciative of her sensitivity to my limited missionary budget, I graciously thanked her but did not immediately accept her invitation. Her generosity was amazing! I really did not want to wear a borrowed wedding dress. I wanted to have my very own.

The following day she called me at Gil's home and reiterated the offer. I thanked her for her generosity, but secretly I had a plan and a strategy. In response to her gracious suggestion, I mentioned that I would do a fitting. Providing her wedding gown did not need even the smallest alteration, I would accept her offer. Phyllis graciously agreed. I knew I was safe. I would return to Winnipeg to buy the gown that I had chosen.

Well, I could not imagine that there would be two women in the whole wide world who had exactly the same measurements! Nothing, absolutely nothing needed to be altered! The dress was simply exquisite and I loved it. My choice in Winnipeg was simplistic and within my budget, but this gown was breathtaking!

God orchestrated details above and beyond my dreams. He provided a wedding dress that was more beautiful than I could ever have afforded! Again, I experienced the amazing goodness of God, when I relinquished my plans and accepted His.

Not only was a wedding gown borrowed, but two bridesmaid dresses were offered by a dear friend, also cognizant of and sensitive to a missionary budget. She offered the attendants' dresses from her recent wedding. You guessed it—the two dresses fit perfectly.

Our wedding day was memorable and wonderful and filled with blessings, one of them quite unusual. The vows had been said, the rings had been exchanged, the special music had been sung and the message given. All was going as planned and only the dedication prayer remained.

As we knelt, our pastor prayed and asked God's blessing on our marriage. That was good! He then added one more request and prayed, "And Lord, please help Gil to become more fluent in Spanish than Jean." I was not only shocked at his un-wedding-ish prayer request, but as we knelt my thoughts were, "Why, I have already been speaking Spanish for six years and am fluent in the language. It is inconceivable that Gil would ever become more fluent." To be honest, I was somewhat ticked.

Following the wedding ceremony, the reception line provided the opportunity to personally meet our loving family and friends. Going through the reception line, a dear friend congratulated us, then added, "Jean, I can't believe that having been single for so long, you got such a handsome man!" Well, my goodness, I didn't think I was that old, but I was indeed thankful for such a handsome husband!

To conclude a wonderful celebration of God's goodness, the Women's Missionary Fellowship of Woodrow Gospel Chapel joyfully provided and served our wonderful guests a sumptuous complete course meal. Following a honeymoon in the Alberta Rocky Mountains, Gil completed additional classes at the University of Manitoba, squeezed in between deputation meetings.

Six months later, we arrived in Panama in time for our first Christmas together.

Significance of a Second Missionary Term

Church Planting in Santiago de Veraguas

BEFORE LEAVING CANADA WE RECEIVED WORD THAT OUR FIRST ASSIGNMENT AS A married couple would be in the city of Santiago. Within a week after our arrival, we moved to Santiago and joined another couple in this interior educational city in the province of Veraguas.

Albert and Esther, Mary and Dorothy were the first missionaries assigned to Santiago. They arrived in 1955, which coincided with my first assignment in Campana. Later George and Esther replaced them, and in January of 1963, Gil and I joined them in establishing "La Iglesia Evangelica de Calle 9" (Evangelical Church on 9th Street).

Four months after our arrival, Gil preached his first sermon. It was a stellar moment. He was a gifted linguist who spoke Low German, spoke and wrote High German without difficulty and had an ear to discern and mimic pronunciation. Gil was not shy or introverted; it was easy for him to laugh at himself when he made language mistakes. He was focused and disciplined; to facilitate language learning Gil formed relationships and played Scrabble with students attending the Teacher's College. Gil did become more fluent in the language. He shone.

In a letter to his parents and siblings on April 25, I wrote,

> On Good Friday we had a special service with the choir singing. Gil sang a solo, "Thirty Pieces of Silver." That morning Gil taught his first Sunday School class in Spanish. In spite of the few lessons he has had, he is learning very quickly. He has

brought the meditation twice in Prayer meeting and will be sharing his testimony and giving the message next Sunday.

In retrospect, Gil also skipped the stages of culture shock. He never became negative or isolated himself from the people. Thanks to my pastor's honest prayer and Gil's diligence in learning, his ability in Spanish was exceptional. I am grateful for honest prayers, even those uttered in the most unexpected places and circumstances!

The Births of Our Children

While we were in Santiago our two children were born. A wonderful Christian doctor in the American Canal Zone delivered both of our babies. We were also blessed by the gracious hospitality of Canal Zone friends while we waited.

Gil's parents and brother arrived from Canada in time to celebrate the birth of a new grandchild. A missionary couple who would be out of the country for a few weeks offered their apartment in downtown Panama City to Mom, Dad and Lawrence. God provided one more time!

January 8th, 1964, was a never-to-be-forgotten significant day! That evening God blessed us with a beautiful son. We named him Glen Alan. The birth went well and I was back in my room when, outside the window, we saw unrest begin to foment. Gil was in the hospital room with me. The American flag had just been burned. Youth who were in the hospital parking lot began to destroy cars. We watched it happen. Gorgas Hospital was only a block from Tivoli Avenue, the street that divides the American Canal Zone and Panama. The 1964 revolution and its riots had just begun.

Hatred for the Americans and fury towards the USA spilled over into violent riots. We were trapped. The hospital was in a blackout. Gil could not return to our friends' home. Gil's parents and brother could not leave their apartment in Panama City. Snipers were on Ancon Hill just behind the hospital. Medical staff could not go off duty and new staff could not come to work.

I shared a hospital room with a young mother whose husband was in Vietnam. She was alone and terrified. The Vietnam War and

Panamanian anti-American riots were reality. And, we had just brought two new babies into this world of rage and death.

While in the hospital we had no idea that young revolutionaries were pouring into the Capital from all over the country, some of them from our city of Santiago. They joined mobs already casting rocks through windows, throwing Molotov cocktails and agitating in the streets. From our hospital room we heard it all. They were expressing their utter fury for the American people. When those young men returned to Santiago, some were horrified to discover that stones had been pelted at our house. One of them was reported to have said, "You can't throw stones at Don Gilberto's house. He is my friend." It is all a matter of perspective.

A few days passed before Gil could negotiate with the Panamanian police to escort Mom, Dad and Lawrence to the Canal Zone. During that time, neighbors who knew that Canadians were trapped in the apartment building graciously extended care. Strangers became friends and concern was genuine. Meals were provided. Assurance of safety was given. God was providing again!

Upon discharge from the hospital, baby Glen, Gil and I were invited to stay in the Canal Zone home of a Costa Rican couple, whom we were yet to meet. Two weeks passed before we could return to Santiago. Glen entered this world with a flurry of activity and fanfare unlike any other we had experienced. During the revolution we became very much aware of what it means to belong to and be blessed by the body of Christ.

Six weeks later I was scheduled for my checkup appointment with my doctor. I kept the appointment. Both mom and baby were fine. With the examination over, I was about to walk out of the doctor's office when he said, "Señora, we are not finished yet. I have something to say to you." With a congregation of one and a twenty-minute message, my doctor clearly and concisely explained that my role had changed from that of a full time missionary to a full time mom. Glen was now my responsibility. The implications of my new role were startlingly clear.

Glen was born in the dry season, the time of our camping ministry. In the past I had been a big part of pioneering the camp initiative; we cooked all three meals outdoors on three stones and we camped in the

49

guest house, as there was not a dormitory or dining room. It was rugged, demanding and thoroughly effective.

Only weeks after Glen's birth, Gil was ready to drive to the Farm for two weeks of camp without me. I would be staying at home with a new baby, some dirty diapers and a few sleepless nights. I felt very much alone and I became very aware of just how much life had changed. I didn't like it. It was all too new and different. Over the years, I have forgotten many things, but the morning that Gil drove off and left me with a new baby is as vivid as if it were yesterday.

I remain deeply thankful for my doctor. I am grateful that he did not let me out of the office with just an examination. God used him to prepare me for the demands, blessings and requirements of parenthood.

Gil and I soon developed our own family ministry philosophy and practice. It was not a philosophy of hierarchy of God, family, ministry and the dog! From the start we were a team of three. Glen went with us on house visitation and people loved him. He was born at the time John Glenn landed on the moon. So before we knew it, everyone was calling our baby 'John Glen.' Glen became a catalyst and a door opener, beginning his door-to-door visitation very early in life!

Two years later our team of three became a foursome.

Preparing for her birth, we made our way to the guest house at Camp El Amanecer fondly referred to as "the Farm." There we waited. Provision was made for our two-year-old, Glen, to be cared for by a fellow missionary.

It happened in the middle of the night. We called Freida and off we went! At that unearthly hour no one would be on the road, so all would be well. Our car was not entirely without flaws, for at a certain speed it would shimmy. All was going as planned, as Gil was driving at the proper speed so as not to cause shimmy problems. Hence, when red revolving lights began flashing, we were puzzled.

The Police Officer approached our car, with Gil losing no time in explaining our situation. The Officer lost no time mobilizing a convoy. "Follow Me!" was all he said. On went his siren, and with red lights flashing, we were escorted in due haste right to the emergency door of Gorgas Hospital. It bears repeating—God provides.

On March 30, 1966, our beautiful blue-eyed daughter, Elizabeth Louise, was born.

I don't know what it was about our children, but they were not content with just the norm as they made their entrances into the world.

We were so grateful for a wonderful Christian doctor who delivered both of our children. God also blessed us with Dr. Enrique Chi, an outstanding doctor in the city of Santiago, who loved and cared for our children and for us. Making house calls in the middle of the night was not out of the ordinary when needed.

Neighbors, Relationships and Hospitality

As we continued in the Evangelical Church on 9th Street, ministry methodology was never neatly and systematically crafted. It just happened. We simply made ourselves available to God and He brought to us those whose hearts He was preparing and drawing to Himself.

My mind is flooded with names and faces of all generations that God brought across our path. Acquaintances became close friends. I remember them well: a little grandmother who walked many blocks to church with her grandsons in tow, the elderly English gentleman who lived alone, the compassionate doctor, his wife and family, the butcher and his family, the Chinese restaurant owner, college students . . . and then there were the neighbors that God planted beside and across the street.

Upon completion of Gil's language course we moved down the street. Our new home was located directly across from the Teacher's College (Normal School). It was Santiago's educational institution where most, if not all, Panamanian teachers received their training. It was a perfect location! We were close to hundreds of young people. Before long, the word on the street was that the newly arrived foreigner was a Canadian high school teacher. Respect and legitimacy opened doors to friendship with staff and students. It was not uncommon to have a student knock on our door just before classes were to begin, asking for help with an assignment due in a few minutes.

A couple of years later we moved to a new development on the other side of town. The first street to be paved led to the newly built

San Vicente Catholic School. Only one lone house on the entire street had been built and it was for rent. We rented it. Within months another home was being constructed directly across from us. We were excited about our future new neighbors, hoping that the renters would be a family with small children. Our neighbors did arrive, but there were no children.

Four American Sisters of St. Joseph took possession. In one way we were very different, but in another, we were the same in that we had all moved to the city to minister to others. The nuns were beautiful young American women who wanted to live holy lives but dressed differently than we did. It was during this time that Roman Catholic Sisters who entered the convent wore full habits. The Sisters of St. Joseph wore long white habits covering all but their faces.

We had some wonderful visits together, had discussions centered on the Bible and from time to time engaged in a game of Scrabble. Often we ran across the street to borrow from each other whatever was lacking when guests arrived. When their Mother Superior arrived as a guest from the headquarters in Louisiana, they accepted our invitation to dinner one evening.

It was a sad day when we heard that the Bishop was moving our friends to another location.

Immediately after they had moved, the Sisters returned and asked permission to wash their habits in our washing machine. We were happy to comply. A special assignment interrupted the process. With short notice, the Sisters were required to leave the city for a few hours. What about the rest of the laundry? I was more than pleased to finish the task. Well, to say the least, there were those who were not at all happy that Roman Catholic habits were drying on my Evangelical clothes line!

Why do I tell this story? It is simple. We must recognize opportunities to bless and be blessed. Our differences can hinder that course. Our neighbors across the street were simply four young American women whose hearts desired to be near God. I am so grateful that God plans and plants our neighbors. With His direction, we can tangibly express the love of Christ and verbalize the reason for our joy—Jesus!

As we moved to Santiago, the Peace Corp also arrived for two-year assignments. We had the joy of meeting some wonderful Peace Corp volunteers based in Santiago and the surrounding countryside. God had planted a brand new ministry right in our path. Many of these intelligent and creative young people joined our weekly home Bible Studies.

On one occasion we were invited to a farewell party for a Peace Corp Team completing their two-year assignment. At the same party newly arrived volunteers would be welcomed. A highlight of the event was a turtle stew dinner with all the trimmings. We were invited to attend, which was a great honor, although we thought that we might be somewhat out of our comfort zone. With joyful hearts, we would be there! Finding a babysitter for Glen was unsuccessful. We had no choice but to graciously decline the invitation. However, one of the Peace Corp single women insisted that we attend and offered to babysit. The door had now opened for us to attend and honor our friends. We accepted the young woman's offer even though it meant that she would not be present at her own Peace Corp party. It was a very wonderful and comfortable evening.

At midnight we approached the host and thanked him for the evening and were about to leave, when our host made an announcement. He added, "Gil and Jean have a Bible Study in their home each Tuesday evening. If you are in the city, please feel free to attend." His unexpected announcement was a delightful surprise. The following day our dear Peace Corp babysitter shared, "We volunteers of the Peace Corp had decided that if you declined our invitation, we would have chalked you up as holier than us and we would not attend another Bible Study." Wow! That night we thanked God for taking us just beyond our comfort zone.

It was Canadian Thanksgiving in Santiago. We had another week before our financial remittance would arrive from USA Headquarters in Kansas City. Our cupboards were bare, very much like Mother Hubbard's. Really, Gil and I did not have the resources to indulge in a huge turkey or chicken dinner, but the absence of a turkey didn't deter us from inviting Freida and Martha, two Canadian team members, to join us for Canadian Thanksgiving dinner.

Our thoughts could have turned to our families back home. Sentimentality might have set in as we envisioned them sitting down for a huge turkey dinner with all the trimmings. We could have had a pity party and really enjoyed feeling sorry for ourselves; however, we didn't indulge ourselves but instead began to plan for a Canadian Thanksgiving in Panama. The table was set with Royal Albert China, crystal goblets, orchids from our yard and long stem candles in crystal candle holders. The menu consisted of rice, pork 'n beans and a tossed salad.

It is interesting that, at my age, I have forgotten many a Thanksgiving—and I have had many! That particular Thanksgiving dinner in Santiago remains a memory forever etched in my mind. Royal Albert and crystal replaced Melmac and plastic. The missing "traditional bird" did not deter us from being grateful. Amazing how good our dinner tasted that night!

A few months had passed since that Thanksgiving, and Christmas Eve had arrived in Santiago. By midnight every one would be on the streets embracing one another and extending invitations to their homes. Delicious goodies were cooked and baked, ready for the Christmas Eve festivities that would, indeed, last all night. Because we would be indulging in many calories and sweets later on in the evening, leftovers were on the menu for supper. Then, the unforeseen happened.

Unexpectedly, one of the Peace Corp young men whom we had invited to stop by anytime did just that! I was stumped. What could I possibly prepare and serve? There were leftovers . . . but just enough for the two of us and no more. We invited him to join us for dinner. While Gil visited with him in the living room, I was in the kitchen frantically wondering what to serve. So I took "the simple route." We sat down to a meal of toast, peanut butter and jam. That was it.

As we ate our meager meal of toast, he kept repeating, "This is the best meal yet. I am so tired of rice! I have had such a craving for just toast with peanut butter and jam. You could not have given me anything that would have made me happier."

I just about missed it! Just about missed out on the blessing God had for all of us. The temptation to entertain and impress can be a trap,

54

a trap to rob the blessings of simple hospitality—like blessing a young American man far from home on Christmas Eve.

Sometimes an invitation to one's home can change the course of one's life. It was about to happen. While living in Santiago one of our many delightful guests was a Guatemalan evangelist. After reviewing the blessings of his time in Panama, he said, "I do not understand you missionaries. Your strategies of evangelism and discipleship do not include the professional class. Do you really believe that the professional class does not need redemption?" Well, that was all Gil needed. Immediately he began research, only to discover very few were ministering among this social class of people. God opened our minds and hearts to the possibilities of a new ministry and an expanded vision.

Misunderstandings Become Mountains

Gil and I remember wonderful times of blessing during our years in the city of Santiago. Ministry, however, was not without its struggles. Some were significant enough for Gil to sense that we best not continue as missionaries. We were in circumstances which proved to be both painful and difficult. Within time we decided that, because of the situation, it would be best to resign and return to Canada to teach.

Gil wrote a letter of resignation to our President, Don P. Shidler. Upon receiving our letter, he immediately booked a flight to Panama to investigate and explore the meaning behind the resignation he had just received. He asked to meet with several parties for transparent and honest discussions. Without our knowledge, another couple serving in another ministry had also resigned. He would not accept either of our resignations.

It became noticeable that Satan, the accuser of the brethren, can take small misunderstandings and build mountains! His obvious scheme was to defeat and discourage missionaries to the point of resignation. Had it not been for the loving care of our President, who took the next flight to Panama, the devil would have been successful! We were profoundly grateful for Dr. Shidler, a godly leader who firmly believed "Missionaries are too valuable to lose."

55

Near the completion of our term in Santiago, Al and Tish arrived to join our church planting team. From the outset of ministry together, we asked God to keep us accountable to Him and to one another. God truly put a deep love in our hearts for each other. It is interesting how Jesus says that it is obvious for others to know if we are His disciples or not. It is all about love. In John 8:35, the apostle John said, *"By this everyone will know that you are my disciples, if you love one another"* (NIV). People in Santiago were watching us and the church grew.

A Change in Ministry: From Church Planting to Theological Training

In due season, Gil was asked by the Field Council to become the Director of Bethel Seminary, located at the Farm. An unexpected move became part of the plan. Gil, who was a gifted teacher, anticipated this change in ministry with great excitement. Leaving the city of Santiago was tough; we had made so many friends and we saw God at work. Yet, in all of this, Gil could not erase from his mind the words of our Guatemalan friend.

Transitioning to New Ministries

Appointment as Director of Bethel Seminary

MOVING TO THE CAMPUS OF BETHEL SEMINARY ON SUNRISE FARM WAS LIKE COMING home for me. the Farm was where it had all begun, and now I was back, moving into the same house where I initially got my start.

Elim Academy, the elementary school for the missionary kids had moved from the Chame campus, where my brother in law Cliff was the teacher. Elim relocated to the Farm. Alvira, the elementary school teacher had arrived, and Gordon and Ruth became the Dorm Parents. Our children now could live at home and attend school only a few steps down the path.

Teaching was Gil's gift. He loved the classroom where he taught courses in Bible, Theology and Music, led the seminary choir and formed a male quartet. Gil loved interaction with students, being engaged in their lives both in and out of the classroom. Our home became the center of many coming and going. In letters written home he often mentioned how teaching energized him. Gil was in his element.

After a few years of directing Bethel Seminary, a decision was made to close the residential school and transition to "Theological Education by Extension." TEE was a program founded by Dr. Ralph Winter, a strategy to take the seminary to the students rather than bring the students to the seminary. Within a short time, six extension centers were functioning with fifty-four students enrolled. This was ten times the number who had applied for residential study.

Guest House Ministry

The original owner of the Farm had built a small house at the end of the extended driveway lined with palm trees. We understood that he had built it specifically for his hired help. I envisioned this little house becoming a GMU Guest House. I thought it would be a perfect place for weary travelers. I set to work and washed, scrubbed and prepared the three rooms and two bathrooms. Within months, the Guest House was ready. There was no need to advertise or put out a shingle, as guests just began to come. Rental prices were incredibly low regardless of how long or short the stay. They came. They blessed and were blessed. They left their "heart prints" on our doorstep.

Attempting to adequately describe hospitality at the Guest House would be impossible! To give you just a small glimpse of the ministry, the following are a few separate random entries from my letters written home.

Shirley left the Guest House just like she found it; had all the beds remade and the floors washed. Within thirty-six hours after they left, the Guest House was completely filled again. Jess landed along here at ten at night without reservations. Another car pulled in and the driver said, "Can we stay in your guest house? I didn't have any idea who they were but gave them a room, and later discovered they were missionaries from Honduras who had come to Panama to buy some equipment. They left at four in the morning.

The Guest House is full again. Today besides routine duties, I washed all the Guest House sheets and towels, ironed the sheets and made up the beds again. I am bushed.

Next week we have a family coming to spend ten days, plus missionaries and their guests are visiting from Canada. When they leave we'll get the place clean, the beds changed and ready for a couple arriving from Argentina. We are expecting others here for Christmas plus another two couples in January from Canada.

A couple from California are traveling around the world and are camping here until they can find a ship to take their car to Colombia. Another couple has just arrived, who have come to Panama to inquire about a possible ministry here.

A "man on a horse" arrived as he is traveling around the world on horseback. He has 'parked his horse' for the night. The other couple has just left. Jake, the man on the horse came for supper, had a shower and will go to church with Gil. Jake is from Switzerland but has spent a few years in B.C. and then attended a Lutheran Bible school on the prairies. We have been so blessed by this fine Christian man.

When everyone finally left, I got the dishes done, the children bathed and devotions were over, when another missionary couple arrived. I just went with them to make up an extra bed. Just finished getting them settled when another missionary couple arrived, I got their beds made and back to the house. It has been a round of lunches for everyone. What a day!

Missionaries en route to Argentina are here with their four children, with plans to leave tomorrow. However, their four-year-old son was in severe pain, having fallen off a swing. His parents have taken him to a physician in Panama City who has diagnosed him with a tumor. He has urged them to get to the States immediately; he has made an appointment with a surgeon in Miami to see him. My heart was so touched at the airport with the attitudes of the three children being left behind. There was no complaining and even though they have just met us for the first time they are quite content to stay with us.

The guests from California are still here. He built a tree house for the kids in one of our large mango trees. Tonight his wife invited us for a supper of rice and chicken in the tree house. What an experience for all of us to climb and eat supper together high in the mango tree! They have been here three months, but plan to leave next Wednesday for Colombia as they continue their trip around the world.

A family with four daughters has arrived. We were absolutely amazed at how each of their daughters looked so much alike, only to learn today that each of them is adopted! They have been missionaries for a number of years and while on each of their four furloughs, they adopted one more daughter.

At the end of a very full day, I dropped on the sofa and breathed in the fresh evening air of the tropics. Washing sheets and towels, remaking beds had been the order of the day. It was now ten o'clock, and just as I was thinking to myself, "I'm too tired to ever get off this sofa!" a car drove into the Farm. We have screen windows and doors. I let out "Oh no!"

A family came to the door and the gentleman asked, "Who just said, 'Oh no?'" Well, I had been caught in the act.

Although they had not made reservations, they asked if they could stay the night. I did get up off the sofa and found a couple of cots and a bathtub in the storage room. They got the cots and the baby got the bathtub. Finally, everyone was settled down for the night. The next morning, one of my guests said, "Well, Jean, you should have been around when Mary and Joseph needed help!"

Guests. They arrived as strangers. they left as friends. They encouraged and blessed us. Now, six decades later, many of them continue to be treasured friends and the blessings continue.

Bible Studies with Urban Professionals

Why are so few serving Christ among the urban professionals? was the question that kept coming to mind. Was this Guatemalan leader the one whom God would use to take us in a direction that we had not anticipated? Being raised in a rural setting and sensing our own inadequacies, we asked ourselves, "How can we possibly cross into an urban culture?" We were content and happy in just continuing to do what we liked best—teaching and giving hospitality.

One particular morning my personal perspectives were challenged, when the wife of a diplomat at the American Embassy unexpectedly arrived and clearly shared the purpose of her visit.

Beryl told of the weekly Wednesday Bible Study held for the spouses of the Military and Diplomatic Corp. She had driven out from the Canal Zone with a specific purpose in mind. She got right to the point, asking me to be the Bible Study teacher. My first response was, "No, no, no! I would be totally out of my comfort zone, and I quite like my comfort zone!"

Having grown up on a farm in southern Saskatchewan certainly did not prepare me for understanding military protocol. Beryl would not let me off the hook. She explained that these attractive women had everything but Jesus and a knowledge of the Word of God. There was no need for more prayer or for more time to make a decision. I knew what I needed to do. I agreed to be at the Bible Study the following Wednesday!

Paul's letter to the Romans was our focus. I prepared and studied for hours! I prayed as never before! Then I stepped aside, got out of the way and waited to see how God would work. When one is so weak, one becomes incredibly dependent on God. It is a good place to be! I recall hearing my dad saying, "It is a great life if you don't weaken, but greater if you do!"

I am encouraged by the apostle Paul's words in 2 Corinthians 12:9–10, *"Therefore most gladly I will rather boast in my infirmities, that the power of Christ may rest upon me. For when I am weak, then I am strong"* (NKJV).

In her devotional book, Jesus Calling, Sara Young puts it this way: "When you depend on Me continually, your whole perspective changes. You see miracles happening all around, while others see only natural occurrences and coincidences. You accept weakness as a gift from Me, knowing that My power plugs in most readily to consecrated weakness."[6]

Week after week, I experienced strength in my weakness as I led lovely professional women in an inductive study through the book of

---

[6] Sara Young, *Jesus Calling* (Nashville, TN: Thomas Nelson, 2004), 257.

Romans. When I got to the third chapter, I wondered how they would respond to the truth of Romans 3:23, *"For all have sinned and come short of the glory of God"* (NIV). This was God's truth, not a personal opinion. Calvary is the story of redemption. The truth of the Word was personally being discovered, and for some it was for the very first time.

As the weeks went by, it was not unusual to get a phone call and hear, "I accepted the Lord at a red light on the way home." Another would call to say, "I just now accepted the Lord in my living room." They were welcome words to my heart! We were all learning to personally discover and apply God's truth to our lives.

Several of them had not ever audibly prayed in public. We began with just two or three words in audible prayer, such as, "Thank you, Jesus." That was sufficient. Soon there were those who were comfortable in sharing their prayer concerns. Some requests were very personal, others incredibly painful. As time went on, prayer became an essential part of Wednesday mornings. We had become confidants, feeling comfortable with one another as we shared heartfelt needs and hurts. Our Wednesday morning Canal Zone Bible Study became known as "the study where the coffee pot and the Kleenex box are passed at the same time."

Marilyn Romaneski, the spouse of a military officer, shares those early days in the Canal Zone with her perspective of our weekly Bible studies.

I was floored when my husband got military orders to the Panama Canal Zone in 1972. I was forty-two and in my prime. Al had a responsible job at the Pentagon. Life was good. For the first time in my life I cried huge buckets of tears at the thought of uprooting. I didn't know it then, but God was beginning His job of reshaping me into His image by saying, "Go. I'll be with you all the way." On the first Sunday in the Canal Zone we met Gil and Jean Reimer.

They were not at all like my idea of what a missionary should look like. I had known only one missionary before, a godly and able fun loving woman, with her Revlon-free lips, and ankle sox and brown oxfords, she fit my idea of a typical missionary. Every five years she returned on furlough with great stories of her life in the far away African jungles.

Shortly after we met the Reimers, I learned that Jean led a Bible study for Canal Zone women. Something or Someone pushed me out the door the next Wednesday morning. I found myself in a crowded room of seeking women and Jean in the midst of them, leading them, delving into the Scriptures verse by verse. Later in the year, when our hostess moved away, I volunteered to have the women meet at my house, a centrally located place with a spacious living room overlooking the Canal. God had set my life on a course. It was His course and the one which He had in mind for me.

That Bible study became my lifeline. Jean was faithful to deliver God's life-changing words straight from the Source each Wednesday. As I look back, that weekly gathering became a major changing point in my life as well as in others. Many personal catastrophes happened during that time, including one of my own, and we were there for each other for encouragement and support.

Thank you, Jesus, for using the weak things of this world.

Monday mornings at the Farm became significant and rewarding. MaryLee and Ben, who were serving at Radio Station HCJB, lived only a few miles down the Pan-American Highway. MaryLee and I developed a close friendship, and because of diverse circumstances that only God could heal or fix, concentrated prayer was imperative. Schedules were cleared for Monday morning prayer. Often, petitions and intercessions came from hearts that were heavy and sometimes broken. God met us in our honesty and transparency. Apart from Him, it was evident that we could do nothing. We asked—He answered! The interesting thing is that others saw the answers too!

Thank you, Jesus, for Monday mornings with MaryLee.

The Man in a Brown Suit

One afternoon, a cordial and well dressed man in a brown suit showed up at the Farm. My husband was away and I had not seen him walk down our long driveway. His visit was intentional. He was looking for Gilberto Reimer. He understood that Gilberto was a noted Bible teacher from whom he wanted to learn. He added, "I do not want to be a Pentecostal, a Methodist or a Baptist. I just want to study the Bible. Where is there a Bible Study that Gilberto teaches?" I gave him the address of the home in Panama City where we met for Bible Study. Somehow, his craving for the Word did not seem authentic. I did not expect to see "the man in the brown suit" again.

Urban Church Planting Strategies

Our missions organization had been in the Republic of Panama for thirty years, with an initial ministry strategy of establishing churches in small cities, towns and villages in the interior. Now, the vision and focus was expanding to include an urban ministry in the country's capital. To accomplish this, it was imperative that we live among them. Where and how?

The possibility of renting an apartment would be financially beyond our budget. However, the search began. An apartment on the sixth floor of a high-rise apartment building was discovered. The price was more than we could pay, but not more than the Lord could provide, and provide He did! Each floor had only two well designed apartments covering the length of the building. We shared the entire floor with a couple of Jewish and Asian origins. It didn't take long to become friends, trusting one another with our house keys to water the plants when either of us would be out of town.

Now it was time to turn vision into motion and put feet to our prayers for reaching the urban professional class people. It soon became evident that it would be best for Gil to secure a faculty position at one of the high schools. God, who placed the idea in our minds, provided the position. Gil was interviewed and hired by San Marcos High School to teach classes on religion twice a week. What a wonderful opportunity! Gil and San Marco were a perfect fit.

Gil's classes at San Marcos had begun and we were anticipating our first Bible study. However, we had not yet personally met anyone who shared the same vision and would like to host the weekly Bible study. But God was already ahead of us. He was orchestrating not only our steps but also the steps of Eduardo and Aggie Mellado. Eduardo, a professional engineer, was working for a US company under contract with the Government of Panama. With their four children, they began attending Balboa Baptist Church in the American Canal Zone. A friend asked if they would consider hosting a Bible Study in their home and later introduced the Mellados to us.

Engineers and Mexicans whom our hosts had become acquainted with at work and through the Mexican Embassy were the first ones to attend. Gil began with an inductive study of the book of Colossians.

"Given to hospitality, apt to teach" (1 Timothy 3:2, KJV), two of several qualifications for an overseer, became the basis for our strategy. Qualifications given by the apostle Paul for church elders is indeed a strange biblical passage for a church planting strategy! Somehow, it gave direction and provided a strategic plan.

God had given us the spiritual gift of teaching. Classrooms and students energized us. "Apt to teach" was one strategy, but what about "given to hospitality?" So our plan included an invitation to dinner to each one who was attending the Bible Study. Many full course meals were prepared and consumed, followed by coffee and dessert on the terrace. As we sat around the dining room table, we enjoyed hearing stories of their families and heritage. They loved telling them, and we loved listening. It was evident they appreciated the evening. Isn't it true that we usually have the best time when we get to share our stories with one another?

One of Gil's many pastimes was to memorize encyclopedias. Strange, but brilliant! He was well read and knew the history and culture of many countries, including the countries represented around the table. I recall how astonished and delighted our guests would be as Gil would interact with them on topics related to their countries of origin. On more than one occasion before coming for dinner, there were those who had made personal decisions to no longer attend the Bible Study. Somehow, over the course of the evening, they would change their minds . . . we like this guy, think we will continue to show up!

During the next two years one Bible Study turned into six. Each study was unique in nature and specifically designed for those in attendance. All the studies were inductive in method, but no two were alike. Gil was especially delighted and surprised when a few university students asked if he would lead a Bible Study specifically designed for them. Although Gil's schedule was already full, he accepted their invitation to teach the Scriptures each Saturday afternoon. As we facilitated each study we were all personally discovering truth, some for the first time.

What about the "man in the brown suit"? Did he ever follow through on his request for Bible knowledge? He did. Immediately following his visit to the Farm, he sought out the hosts at their Panama City address. He attended faithfully. Before each study he would remind us all of his poverty and his very limited education and then lament about the dysfunctional government.

After one Bible Study, he made a confession of faith. He asked Gil if he could also enroll in one of the three levels of "Theological Education by Extension" courses. Because of his limited education, Gil strongly suggested that he enroll in the first level. The "man in the brown suit" insisted that he begin at the most advanced level. Interesting! Interesting the reality of how well he understood the content, and how well he was able to complete all his lessons. For someone with very little education, he surprised us all.

Plans for a Three-month Home Assignment

It was January, 1974. The rains had stopped, the dry season had begun and camps would soon be in full swing. the Farm, with its dorms, dining room, swimming pool and meeting place, served as the center for all camp programs and activities. Squeezed in between camps and Bible Studies, we took time to compose a much-needed newsletter.

We wrote about several things, including plans to be in Canada during the months of June, July and August. We wrote of God blessing the Bible studies, with the hopes they would be combined to form a church in the fall. So confident we were of what God had in mind that we included Romans 12:12 (NLT) *"Be glad for all God is planning for you,"* a verse read in our family devotions that day. Our newly composed and edited newsletter was off to the printers.

We knew what He was planning. We had no doubts about our future. We would spend three months in Canada, and upon our return we would establish our first church. The "man in the brown suit" was very enthusiastic about combining all the classes into one congregation. He offered to initiate a search for an appropriate meeting place and promised that he would have a potential location by the time we returned.

Gil accepted the invitation to be the Bible teacher at two consecutive camps on the Atlantic side of the Isthmus. Following his two weeks of camp, I was to spend a week at the Farm helping direct a young women's camp. Plans were to continue with our routine of Bible studies and Theological Education by Extension (TEE) classes until the end of May. Dry season was always a busy time as we attempted to keep a schedule of home Bible studies, camps and TEE classes.

During this time, our children were attending Elim Academy, the school for missionary kids (MKs) located at the Farm. They loved their teacher and they loved dorm life! Life for them could not have been better. They left on Monday mornings and came home on Friday afternoons. Betti Lou put it this way:

I had what I believe to be one of the greatest privileges a child could have, and that is to be born a missionary kid. My brother, Glen, was two years older than I was, and together we both went to a missionary boarding school.

My childhood was what I thought to be both normal and exciting. Each Monday morning we would be driven to our boarding school. Then on Fridays we would go home for the weekend. The other MKs became our close friends and we loved our dorm parents, whom we affectionately called Aunt Ruth and Uncle Gordon. There were only thirteen of us in the school, and so we were all in one classroom and in one dorm. Our dorm parents would always go out of their way to make each week special in its own way. We all took piano and swimming lessons and then spent the rest of the time climbing the amazing trees just outside our dorm or playing ball with each other. It was like an extended family with eleven siblings; there was always someone to play with. Loneliness was never even an issue.

Gil put a high priority on spending quality time with Glen and Betti Lou on their weekends home from Elim Academy. Regardless of whether we had guests visiting, Gil's children got priority over everything and everyone else. Some Saturdays were spent bowling together as a family, visiting a park or just sauntering down Panama City's Avenida Central window-shopping.

I recall one such Saturday when our family had spent some time in the city just browsing. We leisurely meandered down the Avenue as we window-shopped, taking time to look at everything. It was on one of these leisurely morning strolls that I noticed a simple and elegant garnet ring in the window of a jeweler's shop. It definitely caught my attention, as garnet is my birthstone. We walked in, just for fun, and asked the price. The short heavyset store manager wanted a sale. In his strong German accent, he urged us to accept his proposal—just $5.00 a month and we could have it on installment plans. We left, without a commitment or leaving a five dollar bill.

Later on in the week, while we were eating lunch, I recall a conversation we had about the garnet ring. I remember mentioning to Gil, "Maybe we should have put down $5.00 and asked the sales clerk to put that specific garnet ring on hold."

To which Gil replied, "Oh, when I was in town this week, I dropped by that jeweler's store. It was sold!"

Turning Forty

January 29, 1974, was a day not easy to forget. I would be turning forty! Classes continued as usual and we were blessed to have guests visiting from Cavalier, North Dakota. From my perspective, there was no time to celebrate a birthday! Gil had different plans.

The day began early, with Gil presenting me with a box of chocolates. Strange—chocolates as an appetizer in bed before breakfast? He insisted. I opened the box to discover that one of the gold wrapped chocolates had been tampered with. Gil really wanted me to have that particular chocolate. Trying to lose weight and eating chocolate just didn't seem like a good plan.

It was my birthday, so I would begin with chocolate! However, to my shock and total surprise, there was not a chocolate beautifully wrapped in gold paper but the elegant garnet ring seen in the shop window. I was overwhelmed. Gil had a habit of blessing me with surprises! Nothing more was needed to celebrate God's goodness over forty years.

But that was only the beginning. Gil had prepared breakfast to be served out on the terrace with a lace tablecloth, flowers and candles. He served fruit salad and a coffee cake baked from scratch. It was the best! At noon, I was invited to a birthday brunch with Marilyn. No one puts on a brunch with all the trimmings like Marilyn. It was only noon and still celebrating.

Later in the afternoon, our friends from North Dakota insisted on a birthday supper in an elegant restaurant just before our weekly Bible Study. It was a very special evening, but there was no time to linger and enjoy the ambiance and fellowship. Leaving the restaurant, we drove to the home of Eduardo and Aggie Mellado. We had driven to their home every week for almost two years, but then we got lost! Unbelievable! We arrived late, only to discover that all our Bible Study groups had arranged to gather to celebrate forty years of God's goodness! Aggie had prepared a beautiful lunch and baked a birthday cake. I was shocked and without words! Now I understood why Gil had a problem with getting us there on time. I couldn't thank the Lord enough for friends, wonderful friends who just kept on blessing.

Although he had missed several Bible Studies, the "man in the brown suit" didn't miss my birthday party. I thought he was acting rather strange as I saw him eyeing everyone in the room. I mentioned it to Gil, but he chalked it up to my wild imagination.

On the way back to our apartment, I asked our guests from North Dakota if it would be okay if I would just sneak back to my office and work on a Bible Study that I was scheduled to teach in the morning. They graciously agreed, sensing that I needed the time and space to prepare.

That plan was soon thwarted. As Gil turned the key to our apartment, it was filled with our dearest friends from the American Canal Zone, who with one voice shouted "Happy Birthday!"

A total of five parties in one day! With so many friends from so many countries and with so many best wishes, who cares about turning forty? It was the birthday of all birthdays! The whole day was surreal and magical!

Did God, who knows all our tomorrows, have anything to do with this?

Since we are not in the habit of celebrating Ground Hog Day, the second day of February was just another day! We were not even interested in whether the little creature would see his shadow! Tropical weather and Ground Hog's Day have nothing in common! However, when I awoke that morning, I noticed a huge sign on our dresser mirror. Printed in large letters was "Happy Ground Hog Day, Honey!" Beside the sign was a beautifully wrapped little box. Ground Hog Day and gifts just didn't seem to fit! I opened the tiny box only to find beautifully designed garnet earrings to match my garnet ring! Gil surprised me again!

It was such an amazing and perfect gift—but why Ground Hog Day? Was God the only one who knew that Gil would not be around for Valentine's Day?

Together as a Family

As was the custom, Glen and Betti Lou arrived home for the weekend. Although our guests from the States were still with us, the promise to go bowling as a family was kept. Gil never assumed that there would always be more Saturdays. We were not even tempted to take our guests souvenir shopping, and they graciously understood. What Gil promised he kept.

How could we ever believe that there might not be another Saturday—ever!

Monday morning began with Glen and Betti Lou returning to school, our guests flying back to the States, and Gil leaving for two weeks of camp on the Atlantic side. I stayed by "the stuff."

While home alone that week, the "man in the brown suit" phoned a few times. He wanted to know when Gil was going out to the Farm to teach another Theological by Extension Class. He kept asking about the possibility of driving to the Farm with Gil so that he could attend the TEE class, regardless of his many class absences. I told him that the next TEE class would be on Monday night, February 11. He really wanted to go! Because he had missed several classes, I mentioned that he would first have to check with my husband. I also mentioned that Eduardo and his daughters Gene and Birdie would be driving out the the Farm with Gil. "One more thing" I said, "Gil will be alone next week as I will be at camp. Call at supper time to make sure that you can connect with him." It was good that he wanted to resume TEE classes even after a time of absence.

During this time, Dad Reimer had a planned trip to South America with the Manitoba Marketing Board. He suggested that Mom fly to Panama, and at the closure of his business trip he would join her and Lawrence and then fly home together. Noreen, Gil's younger sister, remembers well that decision. She recalls,

> My mom and I were sitting on my red couch in my Saskatoon home, the main floor of the house which housed the Canadian headquarters of GMU where I worked as a secretary, when she talked about her upcoming trip to Panama. She said she hadn't wanted to go because Gil and Jean and Cliff and Diana were so busy and she would just be in the way. One evening Dad said, "Tomorrow you have to decide, because I have to buy tickets." That evening mom prayed for a letter of invitation and got it that very next morning from Gil, begging her to come. Such a direct answer to prayer she could not ignore. How thankful I was later that my mom was there. Even though being in the midst of all the turmoil was very difficult, being at home would have been much harder.

Gil was still at camp on the Atlantic side of the Isthmus when Mom and Lawrence arrived in Panama. Gil could not wait. So, on Saturday night he drove to the Farm to spend an hour with his mom and brother before returning to camp to speak on Sunday. We all looked forward to a good family visit following our weeks at camp. The visit of Mom, Dad and Lawrence was like icing on the cake at the end of the camping season!

Who prompted Gil, after a busy Saturday at camp, to drive a couple of hours from the Atlantic to the Pacific to see his mom and brother for just one hour?

Only God knew about the Monday that was coming!

My parents, Harry and Liz Little

My twin sister Joan and I as three year olds

Campana's street…I lived right around the corner

My home in Campana for six years

My first co-worker Ruth Schjeveland and I in Campana

My co-worker Mary and I in Campana

Engaged with the youth in our Campana home

Gil's parent's, Ben L. and Elizabeth Reimer

Gil and Jean Reimer's wedding on June 16, 1962

Our first prayer card as a married couple

Our children, Glen and Betti Lou, ages four and two

My son and daughter now young adults

Glen, Jean, Betti Lou and husband Bevan

Entance to El Amanecer, Bethel Seminary Centre and Camp property

Our home at "The Farm"… El Amanecer

Gil teaching - doing what he loved best

Gil involved in the music he loved

A few Bethel Seminary Students still serving in 2013: Ventura, Gabriel and his wife Valentina, Navidad, Adan and Abilio

Four special friends from our Ladies Bible Study: Marlene, MaryLee, Beryl, Marilyn and myself

Friend Fred Denton taking time to bless my son Glen in a game of chess

Campana family, still friends 57 years later: Edna, Benedicta and Tuti

God continuing to bless The Evangelical Church on 9th street in Santiago in 2011

*Final picture of Gil, Glen and Betti Lou and myself taken just 24 hours before
Gil's unexpected and tragic death*

Gil's Tombstone in Corozel Cemetery

Our Bible Study hosts Eduardo and Aggie Mellado

Glen, Betti Lou and I shortly after Gil's death

My children and I after our arrival in Canada

Briercrest Bible College campus, our new Canadian home

My husband Alton Barsness and I

Alton's children and now "ours" Berva, Carol and Duane

The Week that Changed Our Lives

Monday, February 11, 1974

IT WAS MONDAY MORNING. GIL HAD JUST ARRIVED HOME FROM THE ATLANTIC SIDE OF the Isthmus. His duffle bag filled with dirty clothes was thrown on the floor. Next to his was my duffle bag packed with clean clothes and ready to go. In an hour I would be out the door and on my way to participate in the final girl's camp for the season.

Before I left, we enjoyed our lunch together. I have forgotten if we had egg salad, tuna or tomato sandwiches, but I cannot forget Gil's comment, "Honey, won't it be good when this week is over and everything gets back to normal? You will be home from camp. The children will be home from boarding school. It will be wonderful to be back to a normal routine week."

How could I possibly imagine that the "norm" would soon be gone forever?

A few hours after I left for camp, Gil also drove to the Farm to teach the Monday evening Theological Education by Extension class. Following his class and before he returned to the city, he came by the camp and asked if I needed anything. If so, he would send it out the next day with Doña Clotilde. Then he kissed me good night and left.

How could I possibly know that embrace would be the last!

I had asked Gene Mellado to share her testimony with the girls at camp, so she drove out to the Farm with her father, Eduardo, and sister, Birdie. Eduardo, Gene, Birdie and Gil drove back into Panama City together. Gene vividly recalls that night.

We took Mr. Reimer to his apartment. As we drove off I looked back to see him walk into his building. I remember thinking of how my parents always wait until we're inside before leaving.

I did not know that would be the last time I would see him alive.

While at camp, I was restless. Sleep evaded me. I had an eerie and uncanny sense that something was wrong. After a sleepless night, a missionary stopped by in the morning. I mentioned that I was concerned about Gil. He rebuked me with, "Oh Jean, Gil is a big boy. He can take care of himself." His "off-the-cuff" comments did not ease the restlessness of my heart.

Unknown to me, that Monday night marked the genesis of four weeks of unexpected personal trials and heart-wrenching pain, changing our lives forever.

Tuesday, February 12

Our dear Panamanian friend Doña Clotilde, who for years helped with the Guest House, graciously offered to continue helping. On Tuesdays she would take a bus into the city, then another bus to our apartment building. That particular Tuesday morning, she took the elevator up to the sixth floor and rang the doorbell, but no one answered. She was puzzled, as Gil knew she was coming. After a few hours of waiting, Doña Clotilde went to the underground parking to check if our car was in our assigned parking stall. Our yellow Renault was not there. Doña Clotilde returned immediately to the Farm and frantically described her day. She couldn't find Don Gilberto!

When Gil did not arrive for the Bible Study on Tuesday night, a serious city search began. They searched the hospitals and made inquiries in as many places as they could. Nothing! Many of our closest friends gathered in our apartment. Someone called the Farm to confirm the news Doña Clotilde had given earlier in the afternoon.

Just as I was ready to teach the evening Bible Study at the camp, Gordon Omland showed up unexpectedly. He took me aside and quietly said, "We cannot find Gil!" I went limp and my Spanish Bible fell to the floor. I felt paralyzed and was unable to utter even one word. As Gordon drove me into Panama City, my mind went wild and my heart was in turmoil. The uneasiness that I had sensed turned into a full-blown panic. I couldn't even pray.

Following a quiet drive to Panama City, I walked into our apartment only to discover that it was filled with many of our closest and dearest friends. I was overwhelmed by their love and care, but I had no words. I paced up and down the length of our apartment and couldn't drink enough water! Relaxing was an impossibility. I was at my wit's end. My husband could not be found!

One of many in our living room was Mabel Wiley, a godly woman whom I highly esteemed and desired to emulate. Mabel stopped me in my pacing, grabbed my hand, and said, "Jean, stop running. Get a promise from God's Word and hang on to it!" I did stop. I grabbed my Bible and asked God for a promise. That evening God gave me the first of many promises.

It was getting late and one by one our dear friends left. I then placed a phone call to the office of Gospel Missionary Union Headquarters in Kansas City, Missouri. They needed to know that Gil was missing. Why would I even imagine that someone would answer? Of course no one would answer—it was midnight in Kansas City and the office was closed! To my surprise, Alan Johnson, our Mission Accountant answered the phone. He had stayed late to work on taxes.

Did God plan this also?

Wednesday Morning February 13

Difficult as the reality was, I needed to make an official declaration that my Canadian husband, Gilbert Abram Reimer, was missing. Canada did not have an official embassy in Panama, so an appointment with the British Ambassador was confirmed, followed by a visit to the Panamanian Police Headquarters. In each case the declarations were identical, but the responses were poles apart.

The British Ambassador took copious notes during the interview, with the assurance that an immediate search would begin. He specifically asked, "Is there any person who knew that your husband was home alone on Monday night?" I gave him the name of "the man in the brown suit." I related the story of my phone conversations with him.

The British Ambassador recorded his name in full and said, "He will be investigated!"

Upon arrival at the Panama Police Headquarters, I reported that my Canadian husband was missing. The officer was nonchalant and it became apparent that this was just a normal part of another routine day. No questions were asked. No notes were taken. The Panama Chief of Police simply said, "Oh Señora, all men have several women. He is out there somewhere, but he'll be back." Emotionally, I was a mess! He encouraged me not to worry, because my husband probably had an affair as all men do, and he would be home in a few days.

Early the next morning, the GMU staff heard the news of Gil's disappearance. Within hours Don Palmer, the Director for Latin America, was in flight to Panama. Don came to encourage, comfort and help wherever possible. He was member care personified!

Wednesday Afternoon, February 13

While I was at the British Embassy and later at the Panama Police station, "the man in the brown suit" stopped by our apartment. He told those at the apartment that he had just learned that Gilberto was missing and was very disturbed by the news. Right after lunch, he rang our doorbell the second time. Trying to console me during his visit, he offered to join the search team and to help in any way possible.

After "the man in the brown suit" walked out the door, I phoned the British Ambassador, requesting that he remove his name from the investigation. I explained that he was a believer and I feared how he would respond to my seemingly unwarranted suspicions. The Ambassador's resolve would not be altered. He said, "His name will not be removed. He will be interrogated."

It was time for supper, but I couldn't eat! Then, the doorbell rang. "The man in the brown suit" returned for the third time, this time accompanied by his Panamanian wife. During their visit, his wife recounted some of the atrocities of the Communist Party for those they kidnap. She explained how some are sent to Cuba, others thrown in jail, while others have their fingers cut off one by one. I am not sure if she thought of herself as a comforter or a realist. Either way, it made for an engaging visit. I wasn't impressed, and it was very disturbing.

Thursday through Saturday, February 14–16

News hit the streets the next day. Headlines of Gil's disappearance covered the front pages of the American Canal Zone, Panama, US and Canadian newspapers. I clearly recall the nausea and horrible dread I experienced whenever someone left a newspaper on the dining room table. Seeing the headlines spread all over the front page was more than I could handle. I would automatically turn the paper over, so the front page news would not glaringly affirm what I already feared.

Throughout the week loving and concerned friends came and went. They prayed, comforted and encouraged us. Wednesday, Thursday, Friday and Saturday were long days. Reviewing God's promises, forming circles of prayer, waiting and trusting described each day. Days were only punctuated by trips to the terrace, watching and waiting for Gil to arrive in our yellow Renault.

As we prayed each day in our Panama City apartment, women in my Canal Zone's Bible Study were gathering every morning at eight a.m. to petition God for Gil's safety and return. Marilyn recalls, "As we bathed Gil in prayer, a peace that passed understanding seemed to hover over our little circle. We knew that God would handle all the details according to His perfect plan."

Sunday Morning, February 17

Early Sunday morning I opened my Bible and asked God for another promise, a promise that would be filled with assurance. Later that day, Dad Reimer would be arriving from Argentina. I desperately wanted a fresh promise of hope with which to greet him.

My well-worn Bible opened to Psalm 68. I began reading—they were verses of victory. My heart leaped. Yes, this was the promise I needed. I read the first four verses:

Let God arise. Let His enemies be scattered;
Let those also who hate Him flee before Him. . . .

> *But let the righteous be glad;*
> *Let them rejoice before God;*
> *Yes, let them rejoice exceedingly.*
> *Sing to God, sing praises to His name;*
> *Extol Him who rides on the clouds;*
> *By His name YAH,*
> *And rejoice before Him.* (Psalm 68:1–4, NKJV)

Amazing! This will be the day! I will rejoice exceedingly in God!

Interestingly enough, as I read the next verse it seemed that God had changed the font. He had not only changed the font but also the font size. He had bolded and capitalized each letter! I read verse five. It wasn't what I had expected, but it was God Himself saying, "A father to *the* fatherless, a defender of widows, is God in His holy habitation. "

In that very moment at six o'clock on Sunday morning, I knew without a doubt that I was a widow and my children were fatherless! I had shared all the other promises with friends and family gathered in the living room. This one was too painful! I could not share it with even one person. I kept it to myself, pondering it in my heart throughout the day . . . "a father to *the* fatherless, a defender of widows . . ."

Sunday Afternoon, February 17

At approximately three in the afternoon, the phone rang. It was a call from the Chief of Police in Balboa, Canal Zone, asking me to come immediately to their police headquarters. The ambience in the room changed to hope. This was the hour everyone was waiting for! All were convinced that the news would be good news.

Friends from Argentina offered to take my brother-in-law Cliff and me to the police station. While I sat in the back seat, I quietly prayed, "Lord, give me the strength and courage to hear the message that You gave me at six o'clock this morning." As I stepped out of the van and onto the sidewalk that led to the Balboa Police Headquarters, a police officer smoking a large cigar met me with these words: "The news is not good."

As the Chief of Police invited me into his office, he picked up a ring and a watch and asked, "Is this your husband's ring? Is this your husband's watch?" I affirmed that both belonged to my husband. He then declared, "Your husband is dead. His body has just been found on the banks of Panama Canal with eleven stab wounds and mutilated beyond description."

Quietly I responded: "My husband is now with his Lord and Savior, the One he loved and served." My mouth went dry and I asked for a glass of water. That was all. We climbed back into the van and in silence drove back to the apartment.

Everything was deathly quiet in the elevator as we moved up to the sixth floor of our apartment building. There were no words and no reason to talk. My shattered heart was lying in pieces all over the elevator floor. Everyone at the apartment believed that Gil would step off the elevator. He didn't.

Our apartment was filled with friends and family all waiting in anticipation. Can you possibly visualize our arrival? An entrance without Gil!

In that moment, I remembered my commitment made twenty years before: "Anywhere, Anytime, Any Cost."

Was this the cost that I had committed to?

What happened next was surreal. Everyone was in shock. Tears began to flow freely. Some began to scream and others started lighting candles. My dear mother-in-law, whose heart was breaking, screamed, "I will never hear his laughter again!"

A former seminary student was sitting on the steps outside the door, sobbing and repeating, "I didn't think they would do it! I didn't think they would do it."

What about my children? How does a ten-year-old son and an eight-year-old daughter respond to their daddy's death? This is their side of the story.

In his own words, Glen describes the week.

I remember being told that Dad was missing. It was Friday afternoon and I was in the shop class. We were each building a small stool, and then Aunt Ruth came and got my sister and me out of class. We sat on the steps of Aunt Helen and Aunt Linda's house. Aunt Ruth told us that our dad was missing and we didn't know where he was but that he was probably in jail. My mind immediately went to the Hardy Boys and how perhaps I could help get him out of jail by getting a message in to him written on invisible ink, etc. I don't remember worrying about any worse consequences.

We went back to our Apartment in Panama City, and waited and waited. Every moment I would think that Dad would just walk through the door and be back with us. There were many people in the apartment and it was a very long forty-eight hours.

On Sunday afternoon, I was out on the balcony playing with some friends. I think that one of them was David and Raquel Cook's son, Adrian. We were playing with a radio transmitter that my grade five Sunday School teacher at Crossroads Bible Church had helped each of us in the class build.

I heard Grandma Reimer in the living room scream something but didn't understand what that was all about. Then David Cook came up to me and said, "Your dad is in heaven." Then I turned and saw Mom and Betts crying in the living room and I went and cried with them.

That evening after people had left, I remember going to the alcove, and I sat down and prayed. I asked God to raise Dad from the dead, arguing that surely that would bring many more people to Christ that way... I had no trouble believing He could do it. I prayed this until the day of the funeral.

I was astonished by Glen's prayer. He was asking God to raise his dad from the dead for only one reason, that many would believe. Was it possible that a young ten-year-old boy was already developing the biblical theology of the lostness of man?

Betti Lou describes this time in her own words ...

It was the second week of February in 1974; I was almost eight years old and Valentine's Day was just around the corner! Our dorm mom had helped each of us girls bake a special heart-shaped cake and decorate it to take home with us that weekend. I could hardly wait to get home and show Mom and Dad my exquisitely decorated masterpiece!

I went to school that Friday morning with eager anticipation for all the promises that weekend held for me. It was on this day, at such a young age, that I learned that God's ways are not necessarily our ways. We knew that very soon we would be free to relish in all the joys that going home for the weekend meant. But we were to also learn that this Friday was to be unlike any other Friday we had ever experienced.

Before the closing bell could ring, Aunt Ruth asked if she could talk to Glen and me outside for a moment. I remember thinking how very odd this was, since I could never remember anyone ever getting pulled out of school before. I did a quick mental checklist and was almost sure I hadn't done anything I could get in trouble for, and I knew my brother, he would never be in trouble! So my curiosity was certainly peaked. She took each of us by the hand and asked us to sit down on the cement step just outside the door. She sat with Glen on one side of her and me on the other, and as I looked out at the palm trees swaying gently in the breeze, her words changed my life forever. Aunt Ruth told us how four days earlier our dad had been kidnapped from our home, an intensive search had begun but he was still missing. She wanted to prepare us that when we got to our apartment, there would be many people there, because everyone was worried and looking for him.

Vannie Jones, my beloved Sunday School teacher, made sure that she was in our apartment when I arrived from Elim Academy. She stood by my side many times throughout the week. She wrote me notes of comfort. She was a special part of my support team.

That weekend was a blur of activity around our apartment in a high-rise downtown in Panama City. The phone was constantly ringing; people were dropping by at all hours to bring food; all I can remember is ham and countless jars of peanut butter. Circles of prayer were being formed all day, praying that my dad would be found. People started flying in from everywhere to be with us.

Then on Sunday afternoon the phone rang again, but this time it was the police asking my mom to come immediately down to the station. My Uncle Cliff drove with my Mom to the police station, while we all waited back in our home, anxious for the news. Hoping against all hope that dad would be walking back in those doors with them. Later in the afternoon, the elevator door opened and I saw my mom alone. My dad was not with her. I remember my mom standing there, and as I saw the look on her face I knew without hearing a word that Dad would not be coming home again. Mom took us in her arms and told us that Dad's mutilated body was found with eleven stab wounds. All I heard were sobs and hysterical crying. I heard my Grandma Reimer cry out, "I will never hear his laughter again!" Everyone was in shock. The room was filled with commotion and confusion. As I looked up at my mom's eyes, seeing her entire peace, I found comfort.

Thousands of miles away, the news had reached family members in Canada. Gil's youngest sister, Noreen, relates the loss and consequent pain experienced from a distance.

It was Friday morning when, during our tea break, my boss, Jake Goertzen informed me of Gil's disappearance. (Apparently Mom hadn't wanted to tell us sisters…we would worry…and all would work out in the end and that was why we only were told so late in the week.) Twenty minutes later I heard it on CBC radio and I realized that this was a serious matter. However, as is typical for me, I pushed aside my panic and told myself that he was just in jail, they would find him, all would be well soon—after all, wasn't half the world praying for his safety?

Sunday came. My dear friend Barb and I attended an evening service to hear our much loved Briercrest professor Dr.

Budd speak. My unease had been growing. An usher asked us to come into the foyer and there Dr. Budd informed me that my brother's body had been found. He prayed with me and spoke words of comfort which I barely heard. Barb and one or two other friends accompanied me home and spent the evening with me while I tried to comprehend that my dear brother Gil was no longer with us.

Gil, the brother that could make me laugh until my sides ached or make me scream at the top of my lungs while being dangled above what I thought was a one-hundred-foot-deep well. The brother who taught me the beauty of classical music and the love of reading; the brother that would feel free to tell me when what I was wearing looked good on me and even freer to tell me when it didn't; this brother, the most influential person in my life, was dead.

Reality struck when the phone in the office rang and it was my dad calling from Panama to talk and to let me know he wanted both Vange and me to come to the funeral. "Do you have your passport?" Passport!

I had gotten the passport for my summer in Panama, a treasured summer with my brothers and their families that I now treasured. So, yes I had my passport, never thinking I'd need it but taking it as it might as well be where I was. Someone knew I would need it. Many times in the days to come, I never once doubted God, who assured me of His love and in spite of tears.

Sunday Evening, February 17

Several hours passed, yet the shock of Gil's death still pervaded the room. We were overcome with grief. We had no idea of any danger that could possibly have been looming. There was nothing that could make us suspicious, except I was beginning to have doubts about the authenticity of "the man in the brown suit." Nothing made sense, no sense at all! There were just no dots to connect. Dots or no dots, one thing was certain, I knew God IS GOOD all the time!

Wonderful friends continued to arrive from everywhere throughout the afternoon and evening. Our living room overflowed with hugs and tears. A sense of shock permeated every corner. We prayed and we cried. One by one our friends left as the evening drew on. By midnight everyone had left, except one. Eduardo Mellado remained. He waited. He had a promise from God to personally deliver.

The room was empty except for our family. Silence had replaced confusion and shock. In the quietness of the moment, Eduardo said, "Juanita, I have stayed until now because God has given me a promise from the Word for you." He opened his Bible to a familiar passage and read from Psalm 40:1–3 (NKJV):

> *I waited patiently for the LORD;*
> *And He inclined to me,*
> *And heard my cry.*
> *He also brought me up out of a horrible pit, Out of the miry clay,*
> *And set my feet upon a rock,*
> *And established my steps*
> *He has put a new song in my mouth*
> *Praise to our God;*
> *Many will see it and fear,*
> *And will trust in the Lord.*
> (emphasis added)

Eduardo left … it was past midnight! I went to bed but couldn't sleep. I thought to myself, what a strange verse to give a new widow. It just didn't compute! Eduardo said that it was God's promise . . . to put a new song in my mouth . . . many will see it and fear and will trust in the Lord. The reality of widowhood had just dawned on me. I was single again. There was no song in my heart or on my lips. I definitely did not feel like singing!

I continued to ponder the promise that Eduardo had shared, and I began to comprehend that personal suffering for the sake of Christ was indeed a "new song." I had not learned even one stanza of a song about identification with Christ in suffering. Also, I was about to learn a new hymn of worship in life and in death.

It is impossible to sing when there is nothing to sing. The new song is a gift placed by God Himself. It was now midnight and God did put a new song in my mouth. Now I must sing, learning a new song one stanza at a time.

Later that week, I learned that the Chief of Police described me as "that women who doesn't have a single emotional bone in her entire body. She didn't fall apart and she didn't become unglued. She only asked for a glass of water. There is something very wrong with that woman."

In response to his comments, I later learned that one of the Canal Zone employees explained the reason "that woman" did not become unglued, hysterical or fall apart. He explained to the Chief that what he had observed in "that woman" was the evidence of the power of God as a result of hundreds of Christians praying for her.

I am in awe of what it means to belong to the family of God.

The Weeks that Followed

The newspapers carried the narrative which had been clothed in mystery, telling the world and revealing the story. The Panama, American Canal Zone, Canada and the Stateside papers reported the story as it unfolded, with random updates such as:

"Family sources said that there had been 'no threats, no enemies.' His passport, wallet and some money was found with the body. According to other sources, the presence of any money lessens the likelihood that robbery was the murder motive."

"Canal Zone police had not amended their original cautious declaration that Reimer 'was apparently a victim of foul play.' Other sources close to the case plainly label it murder."

"Last Sunday afternoon on routine patrol, a Canal Zone prowl car came upon Reimer's body. It was dressed in blue pants, brown shoes and a red-striped shirt. Not disclosed is whether these were the clothes Reimer was wearing at his Bible Study the previous Monday."

"11 stab wounds on pastor's body. Canal Zone police confirmed yesterday that the body found last Sunday beside a lonely road near Palo Seco with 11 stab wounds is that of Canadian missionary Gilbert Abram Reimer, 36. Identification supplied by the Panamanian authorities, Reimer has been a missionary in Panama since 1962."

"Canal Zone police have not disclosed whether they believe Reimer was killed where he was found, or whether the body was taken to the seldom-patrolled road and dumped. It was a little off the road, but not effectively hidden."

"Tuesday, Mrs. Reimer's parents and four other Canadians arrived at Tocumen airport without the correct documentation. When Panamanian immigration learned what brought them here, they were waved through without formalities."

"In Panama with the Reimer case is Randy Harrold, second secretary and vice-consul of the Canadian Embassy in San Jose, Costa Rica. The British Embassy here handles any Canadian matter only until a Canadian official gets here to deal with it."

On February 19, the Kansas City STAR reported:

An inquest into the death of Gilbert Reimer, 36, a Canadian missionary who worked with the Gospel Missionary Union, Smithville, has been ordered by the Canadian External Affairs Department. The body of Reimer, who was last in Smithville two years ago, was found yesterday along the side of a road in the Panama Canal Zone, authorities there reported. He disappeared last Monday from his Panama City apartment. An External Affairs spokesman said the cause of Reimer's death has not been determined. Reimer's home was in Steinbach, Manitoba.

Don Palmer, Smithville, Gospel Missionary Union Vice-president of Field Affairs, said that David Cook, a friend of Reimer, had told him the body showed signs of violence. He said that the condition of the body indicated Reimer had died early this week.

Palmer said that Reimer's wallet, ring and watch were still on the body, indicating that robbery apparently was not a motive in the slaying. When Reimer disappeared February 11, the Canadian department said, it first was thought he was out of town with his wife. When Mrs. Reimer returned later and said her husband was not with her, the British Embassy was notified of his disappearance. Canada has no embassy in

Panama. The embassy in Costa Rica was ordered to send a consular officer to assist in the investigation. Palmer said Reimer had been stationed in Panama since joining the missionary union in 1962. He was one of 16 Gospel Missionary Union missionaries in Panama. He lived in Panama City with his wife and two children."

Surrounded by Love: Grateful for Family and Friends

The date of February 11, 1974, will always be indelibly etched in our minds. It marked the day of God's amazing grace demonstrated by the loving care of hundreds in response to Gil's death.

Within twenty-four hours of Gil's disappearance, a telegram arrived from Dr. Henry Hildebrand, founder and president of Briercrest Bible College, with the promise of Deuteronomy 33:27, "We are praying for you. The eternal God is your refuge and underneath are the everlasting arms."

A representative of the Canadian Embassy in Costa Rica was promptly in flight to Panama to assist in any way possible.

My mom, sister Joan, brother Brian and Gil's two sisters, Evangeline and Noreen, and cousin Del arrived in a few days, having all boarded the same flight in Winnipeg. Dr. Robert J. Reinmiller, our beloved president, also arrived from the GMU headquarters in Kansas City.

Members of the Canadian Parliament, Members of the Legislative Assembly and the Canadian Minister of Foreign Affairs were exceptionally helpful and sensitive to the immediate needs of our family. My parents received several phone calls from Ottawa with the promise to provide help with travel arrangements and to process necessary documents, offering to assist in any way they could.

Government representatives met our family at the Winnipeg Airport, with documents and passports in hand. Upon their arrival at the Panama Tocumen Airport, they were met by officials; they bypassed customs as they were assisted in numerous and unexpected ways. Amazing! For my twin sister, Joan, her flight to attend Gil's funeral was not a total shock. Locked deep in her heart was this story, not shared with anyone ... well, not until now.

Gil's final trip to Panama was on the British ship the Canberra. As a family we anticipated a few days of rest following three busy months in Canada. Joan joined Reimer and Little family members and friends at the Vancouver dock to bid us farewell. Those hours remained secretly etched in her mind.

Joan wrote in her journal, "Good-byes can become normal but never easy. The ship had docked in Vancouver, our family was allowed to go on board for our final farewells. As the ship sailed into the proverbial "blue yonder," my eyes were glued on it until it was only a dot on the horizon, and then no more. A flood of tears coursed down my cheeks, a wretched gut feeling overwhelmed me. I knew I'd never see Gil again! And I didn't."

Now two years later, she said to herself, "Five years on the field, one year at home—that was the policy. But martyrdom?"

The Celebration of Gil's Life on February 21

Interestingly enough, plans for Gil's funeral were discussed a few weeks before his death, when the subject of death was not even in our vocabulary, much less on our agenda. It began in the middle of the week, while seated in a church pew.

An evangelistic crusade in the Balboa First Baptist Church was in process. We attended one of the evening meetings. The evangelist, a gifted communicator from New York, had chosen "Death" as his topic for the evening. He vividly described his "wants" and "not wants" for his funeral when the time came. He said, "I don't want any tears at my funeral. I don't want an open casket with people staring at me! What I do want is the 'Hallelujah Chorus' to be sung, because it will be my Coronation Day!"

As we drove home that evening, we talked about the message. Gil resonated with the evangelist, saying, "That message was great. I also want the 'Hallelujah Chorus' sung at my funeral!" Knowing that his funeral would be years down the road, there was no need to discuss death and funerals. Little did we know it would only be weeks! Yes, weeks later, we were planning his funeral! Gil wanted the 'Hallelujah Chorus'! Would the 'Hallelujah Chorus' from Handel's Messiah even be a possibility? Should I even ask?

Thursday, February 21, dawned with the tropical sun streaming through our windows. We awoke early, as it was the day of Gil's funeral. His grave had been prepared at Corozal Cemetery, the burial place of Canal Zone pioneers, where tombstones are regularly washed—a cemetery with beautiful manicured lawns, stately palm trees, flowers and lush green bushes. Later in the morning our extended family drove to the Corozal Cemetery.

How I dreaded this part of the day! The coffin was not ever opened, as Gil's body had become decomposed beyond description. As we walked towards the burial site, I recall the powerful sense of God's presence and the realization that Gil was not here. His earthly tent had folded and heaven had become his home. Dread had been displaced.

Just minutes down the road from the Corozal Cemetery, we drove to the Crossroad Bible Church. A sound system was also set up on the parking lot of the church for the overflow of guests. Conducted in both English and Spanish, the service was one of exaltation, characterized by hope and victory. Walking into a church crowded with loving friends was overwhelming. The service began and ended as planned.

Dr. Robert Hubbard, Sr., former pastor of Crossroads Bible Church, led the service. Pat Scott served as pianist. Mr. Fred Denton, Chief of Rates and Analysis Branch of the Panama Canal Company and long time friend, read the Scripture in both English and Spanish.

With one voice, hundreds sang one of Gil's favorite hymns, Frances R. Havergal's "Like a River Glorious."

Every joy or trial falleth from above,
Traced upon our dial by the Sun of Love,
We may trust Him fully, all for us to do;
They who trust Him, wholly find Him wholly true.
Stayed upon Jehovah, hearts are fully blest
Finding, as He promised, perfect peace and rest.

Two tributes were given: one in English by Rev. Robert Reinmiller, President of the Gospel Missionary Union with Rev. Don Palmer (Vice President of Field Affairs for GMU) as interpreter, and Señora Hilda de

Guihon, retired Director of Public Schools for the Republic of Panama gave a tribute in Spanish.

Noted Panamanian recording artist Santiago Stevenson beautifully sang in both English and Spanish the last solo Gil had sung on earth, "Solo no estoy, Jesús conmigo está…I am not alone, the Savior walks beside me."

The Word of God was powerfully communicated also in both English and Spanish. Rev. Tom Willey, a close friend of our family and pastor of the Free Will Baptist Church in Panama City, gave the message in Spanish, and Dr. Bob Hubbard in English.

The service ended with the "Hallelujah Chorus." Early in the week, choir director Mildred Hearn sent a call to friends of Gil who had previously sung the "Hallelujah Chorus." The night before the funeral fifty people showed up for the rehearsal. Unbelievable!

As long as I live, I will never forget the congregation of hundreds standing to their feet as the choir sang the "Hallelujah Chorus" from Handel's Messiah with Joyce Morrow at the piano. They sang with tears streaming down their faces and radiating the Christ whom they were exalting!

True to his request just weeks earlier, the funeral of Gilbert Reimer had become his Coronation Service!

Gene Mellado McIntosh, who with her dad, were the last ones to see Gil alive, wrote, "Mr. Reimer's memorial service was the first funeral I had ever been to. We sang, 'Because He lives, I can face tomorrow.' It was an amazing memorial service. God was glorified. I was able to see first hand the hope believers have as they experience death. Christ conquered sin, allowing us to know that this separation by an earthly death was only temporary. Sorrow was defeated by peace and hope."

Marilyn Romaneski, a dearest friend, described the funeral in her words, "People of many tribes and nations were packed into the church and the hallways and the foyer and even into the parking lot. Al and I were part of that great throng, singing, worshiping God and grateful for His grace in orchestrating our move to Panama."

The obituary read as follows:

Gilbert Reimer, third child of Benjamin and Elizabeth Reimer was born on March 31, 1938, at Steinbach, Manitoba, Canada. He was educated at the local country school and received his secondary education at the Steinbach Bible Institute. He then took his training at the Manitoba Teacher's College and entered the teaching profession.

Gilbert accepted Christ as his Savior at an early age and soon afterward dedicated himself to serve the Lord. Feeling the need for more formal education in God's Word, he returned to the Steinbach Bible Institute. Upon graduation he returned to the teaching profession.

In late 1960, when Miss Jean Little was on furlough from missionary service in Panama, they met and became engaged. There were married on June 16, 1962, and together came to Panama as missionaries with Gospel Missionary Union.

Their first term was spent in pastoral work in Santiago de Veraguas, where they made many friends and felt the blessing of God upon their labors. During this time their two children, Glen Alan now aged 10 and Betti Lou almost 8, were born.

During a two-year furlough from 1967–1969, Gil completed his bachelor's degree at the University of Manitoba and upon returning to Panama accepted the directorship of Bethel Seminary, in El Amanecer. Gil found this ministry deeply satisfying and was warmly loved and sincerely respected by all the students and friends of the Seminary.

The next furlough was spent in study, which led to receiving his Master's Degree in Education.

Upon returning to Panama in 1972, they felt strongly called to a ministry of home Bible Studies particularly among the people in Panama City. This work, which began in August 1973, was immediately very successful. The Lord blessed in a marvelous way and many came to hear the message of salvation through these studies.

In the last week before his death Gilbert was involved in a youth camp that brought rejoicing and rededication to many young people.

He met his death early last week at the hands of an unknown assailant and now abides in the presence of his Lord whom he served with sincerity, devotion and faithfulness in a most commendable manner.

His wife, Jean, his two children, parents Mr. and Mrs. Benjamin Reimer, brother Clifford and sister-in-law Diana, brother Lawrence and sisters Evangeline Doerksen and Noreen Reimer survive him.

Also present for the service today are Jean's mother, Mrs. Elizabeth Little, a brother, Brian Little, and a sister, Joan Diener, all from Canada.

The entire Christian community of Panama and the Canal Zone joins in extending their love, sympathy and the assurance of their prayers that the "God of all comfort" will minister in His sufficiency to those who face this deep sorrow and loss.

Following the Celebration of Life service, we walked out into the twilight of the early evening.

Standing alone in the parking lot of the church was a man who obviously had attended the funeral but remained long after all others had left. He approached me, warmly embraced me, and becoming very emotional said, "Now today, for the first time, I understand."

I was shocked and overwhelmed as I recognized him. Evan was a brilliant young man who had previously attended one of our Bible Studies in Santiago. For a number of years, his name had not surfaced in any of our conversations. However, we had learned that he had become a high school professor.

Just weeks before Gil's death, Gil's friend Tom was giving a talk in the high school where Evan was a professor. Following his presentation, Tom was invited to join the faculty for coffee. During coffee break one of the professors asked, "Do you know a Gilberto Reimer? Where is he? I used to attend a study he taught. I have become a Communist leader, so I haven't seen him for many years. Tell him I would like to have coffee with him sometime soon."

Shortly after, Tom mentioned to Gil how he had met his friend at the high school. Gil was not only excited to hear of a friend from the past, but he anticipated the possibility of having coffee with Evan later. He remembered the great discussions they had in Santiago. Evan was a brilliant young man with a keen mind, and Gil enjoyed interacting with him.

A cup of coffee together seated at a favorite café didn't happen. Evan attended his funeral instead.

A few days after the funeral, as we were driving with friends, a Christian radio station was playing a Marsha Stevens-Pino song entitled "For Those Tears I Died." I listened to every word. The last two lines of her song were especially powerful: "I felt every tear drop when in darkness you cried, and I strove to remind you, that for those tears I died."

As I listened, I thought to myself, Oh, I hope that Glen and Betti Lou are not listening to the song. The words, memories and unanswered questions were all too close to home. When, in that moment, Betti Lou looked up at me and quietly said, "Mommy, that is Daddy. God felt every tear drop when in darkness Daddy cried that night."

Words were not necessary, but thoughts of those last minutes that their daddy had lived were constantly haunting us. We attempted to visualize those final moments on earth; how he must have sobbed, struggled and fought for his life, all the time realizing that he might never see his wife or children again! It must have been more than horrendous. Attempting to visualize that dreadful night while at the same time envision God's presence was beyond our human understanding.

It was beyond our comprehension but not beyond our understanding of the specific promise God comforted me with at the beginning of the week, *"He shall call upon Me, and I will answer him; I will be with him in trouble; I will deliver him and honor him"* (Psalm 91:15, NKJV).

Later I was told that God had truly delivered him, as it seemed the first stab wound he received was most likely to his heart.

Investigations and Interrogations

Investigations began by the Panamanian authorities, calling all who had seen Gilberto. Eduardo Mellado was one who was called. Eduardo recalls,

> Since we had taken him to town, we of course were on the police list as persons of interest. I was questioned and told my story. Then they wanted to talk to my daughter. I acceded with the proviso that I would be with her. They agreed. Our daughter, Gene, told the same story and the police seemed satisfied.

For me personally, during these next four weeks, phone calls requesting my presence for government interrogations were frequent. Without exception I dreaded each one, and at the thought, my stomach would tie into knots. The personal focused interrogations by both the Panama and the Canal Zone governments were the most difficult. Two of the interrogations were unforgettable.

Responding to a phone call from the Panama Police, I left my dinner unfinished and drove to the Homicide Building in down town Panama City. The building was old, dark, foreboding and damp! At least, it seemed that way! On this particular early afternoon, my brother-in-law Cliff, who accompanied me, was not allowed to be present for the interrogation.

I was led into a dark room filled with military police and tape recorders. This particular interrogation was very personal and conducted in the Spanish language. The Chief of Police fired one question after the other, giving me no time to ponder or think through a response. The questions were all related to Gil's personal life—the possibility that he'd had an affair or the probability that a jealous spouse had killed him. The interrogation lasted more than two hours. I remained as calm as a cucumber, whatever that looks like!

My serenity infuriated the Chief of Police. He began to scream, saying, "Señora, you are a liar! You know that all over the world every man has affairs. There is no such thing as only one man and one woman. Only God is perfect. Because you are not telling the truth, you are dismissed."

He dismissed me. I walked out. My brother-in-law and I walked out into the tropical afternoon sun. I fell apart and began to tremble. When we got back to the apartment, my mind went wild with possible answers to his questions. I thought of Scripture verses that I should have quoted. Then, in the midst of all this, God spoke into my troubled heart, bringing to mind the words of the apostle Paul in Philippians 4:7 and the words of Jesus in John 14:27,

"And the peace of God, which surpasses all understanding, will guard both your hearts and minds through Christ Jesus. Peace I leave with you, My peace I give to you; not as the world gives, do I give to you. Let not your heart be troubled, neither let it be afraid" (NKJV).

The ability to remain calm in a difficult situation was only God. He was garrisoning both my heart and mind as He lavished His peace upon me. It was the evidence of this peace that made the Chief of Police really mad! God had given peace and I received His gift. I was beginning to understand in new ways the incredible blessings of God. This time it was His peace.

Other lengthy interrogations were held during the weeks ahead. Colleagues were also requested to meet with those in authority. These were trying and complicated days for all of us. We soon learned that our home and phone were possibly "bugged." Consequently, the interrogations became very eerie experiences, as it seemed the interrogators knew every move we made, every trip taken and every conversation spoken. Gil and I had been followed.

We always believed that we lived in one of the safest countries in the world. We had no reason to think otherwise. Prayer for our protection was not a normal or frequent request. However, one afternoon all that changed when I received a phone call from a government official. He informed me that the "man in the brown suit" had been investigated as planned. The investigation revealed that he was a medical doctor, not uneducated and penniless as claimed. Although he often complained about the present government, he served as the Director of the

Underground Communist Party, having entered Panama illegally from a South American country.

At that moment, my suspicions were confirmed. We had a spy in our weekly Bible Studies! He faked a craving for Bible knowledge, a phony conversion and a deceitful excitement for a church plant. He was a fraud and all was a hoax. What could possibly have been the motive behind this weird and bizarre activity that we knew nothing about?

At the end of these four weeks, we assumed that there would be no further investigations. However, that was not the case. Eduardo Mellado tells his story,

Four months later on the first Monday of September, Labor Day, I was going to take advantage of the long weekend and go to Costa Rica to relax with my family. I had been busy and needed some time off.

We were all buckled in our seats when I was called to the front of the plane and was told that I could not leave since there was a warrant that prohibited my departure from Panama. They told me that this was an order from Manuel Noriega. He was then Head of the Secret Police.

We got off the plane and they told my wife and kids that they could go, but of course, they refused. We sat at the terminal for what appeared for a long time and this guard would not explain anything. Finally, late in the evening he just mumbled and told me to accompany him to the police car. My wife and kids followed closely. We reached the police station and my wife went home and I was taken to what appeared to be the officer in charge.

I was told to sit in front of him while he carried on with his own business at his desk ... no explanation came. After a couple of hours he ordered dinner for himself and when he finished eating he said, "I am leaving and you cannot stay here." He took me to a door leading to the basement where the cells were. When I entered that ugly place an elderly gentleman said to me, "No sense to worry about this matter, nothing will be done until Monday when Noriega gets back." This gentleman did not take me to the dirty cells full of people, but rather, led me to a storage area where I spent the night by myself.

The next morning a younger rude character came to me and asked: "Where did you spend the night?" I told him and he said, "You cannot stay there, go there." He pointed to a cell where a whole bunch of people were laying on the concrete floor. Late that evening, one of the characters came to offer me a piece of cardboard to lie on, for a fee of course. I had given my wife all the documents and kept small change with me so I was able to cover the price of the "bedding." Cleanliness was nowhere to be found. Filth was a common denominator.

Sunday, the next morning, providentially some other guard came and told me that I could stay in a hall upstairs where I could see daylight and look out an iron gate.

Eduardo's wife Aggie adds,

We went to the jail, but they would not let us visit or give him the items we had for him. As they did not allow anybody to wait anywhere close, we went outside the building. As we were leaving, Birdie was able to hand her dad a New Testament through the iron gate. Jimmy was so mad; he was kicking the concrete because authorities did not give permission to see his daddy. He was held in jail for seventy-two long hours and released. No explanation or reason given.

Eduardo concludes,

As far as I recollect, this order to restrict my travel out of Panama was given soon after the disappearance of Mr. Reimer and it had not been enforced, as I had left the country on several business occasions. Someone must have been reprimanded for not carrying out the order. So when I was let go, they just brushed it under the rug.

More than thirty years were to pass before we really would know the "why."

Preparations for Leaving Panama

The motive for Gil's death had not been disclosed. It was now certain that we had been followed and every move we made was known. Because I, too, had been followed, it seemed that it was unsafe for the three of us to remain in the country. But . . . where?

Anywhere?

My mind turned back to that night in the gymnasium at Briercrest, when as a teenager I signed a card that read "Anywhere." Where would anywhere possibly take us? What were our options? Many offered their advice and counsel even as they comforted us. We were truly bathed in the love of friends and family who offered helpful advice for the next step.

My brother-in-law and his wife graciously offered an invitation for us to live with them in Panama for the next three months until school vacation began.

My dearest parents-in-law pleaded with us to return to Canada so they could put their arms around us, protect, care and love us.

An American couple living in the American Canal Zone invited us to move to a basement apartment in their home so we could live in safety within the "Zone."

Carl McMindes, President of the GMU Ecuador field sent a letter of invitation for us to transfer from Panama to Ecuador. As gracious as that offer was, it was obviously out of the question. We had never lived in Ecuador. Widows are not to make huge immediate changes. We had heard that there was a waiting list for students to enroll in the Alliance Academy, making it impossible for my children to attend. It just didn't make sense. Everyone agreed that Ecuador was definitely not in the equation.

We prayed. We asked God to show us the next step. We couldn't start packing until we had a destination in mind. Just how does one decide the will of God with so many good options? We talked, discussed and wondered. *"Trust in the LORD with all your heart, and lean not on your own understanding; In all your ways acknowledge Him, and He shall direct your paths"* (NKJV). Proverbs 3:5–6 kept coming to mind. I kept trusting, certain that He would lead. But . . .

Uncertainties prevailed . . .

Where are you and the children moving? Have you made your decision yet? Are there any options, and if so, what are they? These were the questions posed by a friend a few days later, as we chatted in the foyer following a church meeting. We chatted. Within the next few minutes, Dr. Tom Williams made the discovery of God's will appear obvious. His explanations made sense. One by one, he began to review and assess the doors that should close and the one that should remain open. He identified and reviewed the options before me, then explained, "Living with family is a great option, but sometimes it isn't always the best for the long haul. Close that door!

"As much as your parents love you, it would still be a huge adjustment for you and the children to move to Canada. Close that door!

"Living is the Canal Zone isn't even an option, because it is illegal for Canadians to live in the American Canal Zone. Close that door!"

"Ecuador. The GMU has invited you. They have begun the visa process and have offered you an apartment. Even though, there is a wait list to enroll in the Alliance Academy in Quito, the director has extended an invitation to Glen and Betts to register. HCJB, the Christian Radio station has offered you a ministry opportunity when you are able. That door is open, so go through it!"

Ecuador had just trumped all other options.

No doubt you can well imagine the shock of family when I returned to the apartment and announced, "I believe that God is leading us to Ecuador." After everyone got adjusted to the decision, packing began. What God had promised, He was doing, one step at a time. He said, *"I will instruct you and teach you in the way you should go; I will guide you with My eye."* (Psalm 32:8, NKJV). Quite amazing, isn't it? God instructing, teaching, guiding!

Packing began. How difficult it was to take the pictures off the wall and take books off the shelves! Making decisions about all of Gil's items was even more difficult. There were decisions and more decisions. The questions always focused on what to take, what to store or what to give away.

While we were going through this process in our apartment, Glen and Betti Lou were going through a similar process at Elim Academy. Everything was continuing as normal for the students at Elim Academy, except for my children. They were packing up their clothes, cleaning their dorm rooms and emptying their desks in the classroom. Glen put it this way,

> The shock of having Dad murdered and ripped out of our lives was hard. Suddenly now, within two weeks, almost everything else—friends, our home, models, books—was ripped away. I remember only being able to take one thing with me. I was leaving everything else behind…it was tough.

Back at the apartment, boxes were everywhere! As a single missionary, my mom packed my trunks. Never did she or I ever imagine that, twenty years later, she would again be packing boxes for her daughter who was "single again." Bless my dear mom! What an efficient packer! So organized, so perfect, so patient, so loving! Decisions and tears all mixed together. My mom and mom-in-law impressed us all. God blessed me with the most wonderful parents and parents-in-law that anyone could have!

The loving help of friends was unbelievable! I still clearly recall the organized chaos of our apartment, friends and loved ones all helping. Some were preparing meals, others were washing walls, and others were answering doorbells and phone calls. The walls were bulging with God's love, evidenced in every corner through caring friends! I was learning how "God stretches the heart to make room for more and greater love."

Personally knowing God changes everything! He directs our steps, He goes before and He prepares the way. As we packed, I grew in amazement of how Jesus had gone before and was preparing us for a move to Quito, located twenty-two miles from the equator and situated at 10,000 feet high in the Andes Mountains of Ecuador.

Final Days in Panama

The boxes and suitcases were all packed. We were ready to walk out the door for the last time, when the doorbell rang. I opened the door to a lovely young woman who said, "You do not know me, but I live on the first floor in this building. For the past number of days, I have been watching the people as they come and go on to your apartment. One thing amazes me. You all look alike. You all love one another. Can you tell me about your faith . . . I need to hear what you believe." Wow! The first thought that came to mind was the words of Jesus, recorded in John 13:35, *"By this all will know that you are My disciples, if you have love for one another"* (NKJV).

Before I left our apartment, my last God-given assignment was to explain the Gospel to one who had been watching. Our friends were illustrating Matthew 5:16, letting their lights shine before her so that she might see their good works and glorify God. Joy had replaced the sorrow of closing another door for the last time.

Arrival in Quito

Upon our arrival in Quito, Carl McMindes, the Field Director of GMU, graciously offered us a small apartment on the second floor of the office building. That one small room became our bedrooms, kitchen and living room all wrapped into one. We loved it and we were grateful for the closeness we felt in our grief.

Glen and Betts enrolled in the Alliance Academy, where they were received with so much love, where "strangers" soon became friends. My children were again among other third culture kids who understood each other, with experience in crossing cultures, many being born outside their parents' passport countries.

God gave Glen and Betti Lou friends who "understood." Cathy, a former classmate and friend from Panama, had moved to Quito with her parents and was attending the Alliance Academy. Now they were together again. Soon after beginning classes, Glen was introduced to Bob Stuck, a fellow classmate in fifth grade. Even though both were missionary kids, they identified with each other at a deeper level. Bob's dad had also passed away. Both were fatherless. They became friends,

119

and words were not needed to understand each other's hearts. God had done it again!

Life was not without its moments of tears and sorrow. Betti Lou shares her heart . . .

With the flurry of activity immediately following Dad's funeral, those first weeks flew by in a blur. Soon we found ourselves in Quito, adjusting to life with our new smaller family unit.

Within two weeks of arriving in Quito, it was my birthday. My birthday was my absolutely favorite day of the year! The reason being my dad's birthday was the day right after mine. We always celebrated our birthdays together—always! It was OUR special day.

I think that, since we had so many family members and friends enveloping us during the weeks surrounding the funeral, my true loneliness and sorrow didn't come into full fruition until the day of my birthday. Every year for seven years I had always had a VERY special seat while awaiting for my birthday cake—my dad's lap! I would climb on his lap and together we would wait, with great anticipation, for my mom to come around the corner with a cake ablaze with candles for us to blow out together. All of a sudden, that lap was gone! That was my first realization of how much our lives had changed and how much I truly missed my dad. My sorrow seemed overwhelming to my young heart.

In a showing of true Christian love, a group of ten girls whom I had just met but who didn't personally know me, gathered in our little living room and showered me with gifts and love. I may have lost my dad's lap, but God began to fill that hole in my heart with new friends. Those months in Quito were hard yet also special, in that we were ministered to by many who wrapped their arms and hearts around us.

Radio station HCJB extended an invitation for me to join Malcom and Mardelle Brown at the Academia del Aire (Academic of the Air) to work whenever I could. Ecuadorian Director Jose Andrade of Back to the Bible asked me to help with correspondence in their offices when possible. I was so blessed with opportunities to serve with Christian servant leaders who loved me, loved the Lord and were committed to reaching the world through global radio.

The Blessings of Heavenly Mathematics

THROUGHOUT THESE WEEKS, GOD REPEATEDLY BROUGHT TO MIND THE WORDS OF THE Psalmist, *"Bless the Lord, O my soul; and all that is within me, bless His holy name! Bless the Lord, O my soul and forget not all His benefits"* (Psalm 103:1–2, NKJV).

Benefits! My North American culture teaches that benefits come as "additions." I had become accustomed to thanking Him when He added. I could not remember being grateful when He took away. Blessings and benefits come in addition and even multiplication, but never subtractions! Is heavenly mathematics different from the arithmetic I learned in elementary school?

On the eve of our departure for Quito and after the children were in bed, I took out a piece of paper found in my Bible and began to list the blessings when God subtracted rather than added. After completing the list, I placed the wrinkled piece of paper back in my Bible and left it there.

Before writing down even one word, I thought about the losses we had experienced when God subtracted. I had lost my husband of almost thirteen years. My two children had lost their daddy. The three of us were about to leave the country and friends we loved. Glen and Betts were being ripped away from Elim Academy's classroom, dorm and friends. Panama had become very much our home.

Shortly after our arrival in Quito, I took out the little piece of paper that had remained tucked in between the pages of my Bible, reminding me of God's blessings in subtraction.

My eyes fell on the first word written several weeks earlier. The first word on the page was "preparation." God clearly brought to my mind how He had so incredibly prepared the heart of a man, a woman, a ten-year-old son and an eight-year-old daughter.

God Had Prepared the Heart of a Man

As I reflected on the weeks before Gil's death, I was amazed how God orchestrated even the smallest details and decisions.

In one of our urban evening Bible studies, Gil had taught the last chapter and verse of Colossians. He concluded the evening with a question, "What book of the Bible should we study next?" Without hesitation a gentleman blurted out, "Revelation!" Well, Gil looked at me and winked. It was definitely not the easiest book in the Bible to teach new and non-Christians.

Before he could respond with an answer, another had turned to the last book of the Bible and explained, "Look here, it says in the first verses of Revelation, 'Any one who reads this will be blessed.' We cannot miss out on this blessing." The decision was made. We would study the book of Revelation.

Only weeks later, Gil was teaching on Revelation 2:8–11 in the Bible study, focusing on the letter to the persecuted church at Smyrna. Gil read the words of Jesus, *"Do not fear any of those things which you are about to suffer . . . . Be faithful until death, and I will give you the crown of life"* (v. 10, NKJV). How could any of us possibly know that it would be his last Bible study in the city. We now understood that it was God who decided. Amazed . . . again!

Gil's last two weeks on earth were spent speaking at camps for young adults. "Heaven" was the theme of his last two messages. After his death, young people came to my door and talked about his final message on the topic, "Is it worth it all?" which was confirmed by the written outline found in his Bible. He spoke of Daniel, Joseph and Stephen. He described Stephen's death by stoning. He said, "I believe that if Stephen were here today, he would say that even in martyrdom, it was worth it all." Gil Reimer had absolutely no idea that the very next day he also would be martyred—not by stoning but by stabbing. As Gil spoke of heaven, he told the young people that if he were to see Jesus today he would not be ashamed, assured that he was doing what God had asked him to do.

Little did Gil know that he would be seeing Jesus before the end of another day.

God Had Prepared the Heart of a Woman

I was very much aware of my inadequacy to teach the wives of military officers! In preparation for each Bible Study, I literally saturated myself with His Word. I am so grateful to God, who placed me in a situation where dust could not gather on my Bible. I was compelled to be in the WORD. In-depth Bible study prepared me for an unexpected crisis

Several months before, MaryLee and I were meeting for our regular Monday morning prayer hour at the Farm. One morning was different. Before we prayed, Mary Lee told me that her husband, Ben, would soon be transferring to Quito to serve with HCJB Radio. I was devastated! As couples we met for Bible Study and our kids were best friends. In September of 1973, they left for Ecuador and we remained behind.

Three months later on a beautiful tropical evening, our friends Beryl and Bob joined us for dinner. Bob worked in Panama with the Diplomatic Corp and Beryl and I served together in our Bible Studies. After dinner, Beryl and I moved out onto the terrace to enjoy our coffee. It was then that she told me the news. Bob had just received word that he was being transferred out of Panama. This was not unexpected because Beryl and Bob had been transferred many times as they served with the American Embassy. Nevertheless, I was saddened by the news.

Beryl continued, "Jean, you will never guess where we are being transferred?"

"No, I cannot guess."

She could not hold back her joy of sharing the news that Bob was being transferred to Quito, Ecuador. She and MaryLee would be living in the same city again. Bob and Beryl moved to Ecuador in December of 1973. Both friends were gone. I was left behind. How is it possible that two of my dear friends had moved to Ecuador? Without me!

How could I ever imagine that within a few months we would all be in Quito! As our plane touched down on the tarmac, MaryLee and

Beryl were at the Quito Airport to meet us! We were surprised, not so much that we were together in Quito, but amazed that God, who knows all our tomorrows, had totally orchestrated business transfers to make it possible.

God Had Prepared the Heart of a Ten-year-old Boy.

As long as I live I will never forget that Sunday afternoon when we learned the news of Gil's death. After several hours in our living room, my son, Glen, asked, "Mommy, can we go into my bedroom?" Betti Lou and I followed him. Having just learned that he would not see his dad again, I was certain that Glen wanted to just sob and get away from all the confusion, shock and turmoil. Instead of crying, Glen took his Bible off his nightstand and asked if he could read a few verses. He opened his Bible to Philippians 1:1–21. He finished by reading the words of Paul, *"For living to me means simply 'Christ', and if I die I should merely gain more of him"* (Philippians 1:21, Phillips).

With my breaking heart, I cried out to God. "How is it possible that a young boy would know more than the story of Joseph and his coat of many colors or the story of Daniel in the lion's den? How would a small boy know where to go in the Bible in the time of crisis to find comfort for his breaking heart and at the same time comfort his mom and little sister?" How? Because God had prepared the heart of a ten-year-old boy.

God Prepared the Heart of an Eight-year-old Girl.

It was February 21. I awoke with the tropical sun streaming through our bedroom window. My little blue-eyed blond Betti Lou was beside me. "Mommy, this is going to be a good day!" Obviously, her perception of the day ahead was one of limited understanding. "Betts, have you forgotten that this is the day of daddy's funeral?" I asked. Betts assured me that she had remembered and that she knew that it was a day of profound significance. Then she looked up and said, "Mommy, Jesus suffered so much for us. Can't we suffer just a little bit for Him?" What could I say? There were no words or comments, only amazement as I asked myself, "Is it possible that a little eight-year-old has already developed a theology of suffering? How? Because the Word of God had prepared her heart.

The Blessing of His Promises

The advice of my dear friend Mabel Wiley became a continual practice. Many times throughout each day, I asked God for one more promise from His Word. My Bible is marked, underlined and dated. I read, listened and heard the voice of God speaking precious promises to my desperate heart. I soon discovered that when there is nothing tangible to hang on to, His Word is sufficient. His Word became my strength in the times of greatest weakness and despair, and through His promises I was learning to know Him more intimately.

The Blessing of the Prayers of the Church

Along with the blessings of His preparation and His Promises, the prayers uttered by Christians all over the world was more than I could ever imagine. God was hearing our names continually as the Church prayed for us. Telegrams, phone calls and hundreds of letters from across the globe assured us of their prayers. I will never cease to be in awe for the privilege of belonging to the family of God! You have heard me say this before, but it bears repeating. Those without Christ know nothing of this blessing!

A year after Gil's death, I met a lovely Christian woman who approached me and with a delightful accent asked permission to take my picture. Why would she ever want my picture? She was visiting from Italy and related how her church was continually praying for us. She wanted a picture to post in her church. While attending another evening church service, I met a Danish Christian woman. She also told how her church in Denmark prayed every week for us and was continuing to do so. Someone has said, "The definition of a poor man is one who has no one to pray for him." Glen, Betts and I had become the richest people on earth!

The Blessing of His Peace in the Midst of the Storm

On that little piece of paper tucked in my Bible was also the word "peace." The personal interrogations were the contexts where peace was powerfully evident. In those difficult hours, I experienced God's supernatural-beyond-human-comprehension-peace. The Prince of Peace Himself dwelt within.

A bilingual secretary was present in one of the most difficult interrogations, which was conducted in the English language. During those two hours of interrogation, God quieted my heart and mind. Following the interrogation, the secretary asked permission to leave work early. She returned home, threw herself on her bed and wept. A neighbor knocked on her door and discovered her distress. Through tears, she told her neighbor, "I have just experienced one of the worst interrogations ever. That woman has a faith that I do not have, but want." Her neighbor was a believer and led her to Christ that evening.

In our Panama City Bible study, an engineer and his wife attended but did not believe. When I returned to Panama a year later, I learned that they had processed all that had happened. They remembered that Gil taught that Jesus is the answer to all anxieties and fears. After Gil's death, they watched us and they watched Gils's parents. They observed our peace in the midst of a turbulent storm. They told me, "We observed the peace that ruled in your hearts, and as a result, one evening we knelt by our bed and accepted Christ."

The Blessing of His Presence

Jesus promised His presence when I committed my life to a missionary career.

> *"Go, therefore and make disciples of all the nations, baptizing them in the name of the Father and of the Son and of the Holy Spirit, teaching them to observe all things that I have commanded you; and lo, I am with you always, even to the end of the age. Amen."*
> (Matthew 28:19–20 NKJV)

God's presence was promised not only when He called me to ministry, but through difficult times as well. Why was His presence so evident? The words recorded in Isaiah 43:1–2 provides the answer,

Fear not, for I have redeemed you; I have called you by your name; You are mine. When you pass through the waters, I will be with you; and through the rivers, they shall not overflow you. When you walk through the fire, you shall not be burned, nor shall the flame scorch you. For I am the LORD your God, the Holy One of Israel, your Savior. (NKJV)

Twenty years earlier, He promised that He would not abandon me—ever! The promise of His Presence was kept. His Presence was evident. Following Gil's funeral, a new friend offered to wash the dinner dishes each evening. When I asked why, she replied, "I just feel the presence of God so real in your apartment, I want to be here!"

The Blessing of Praise

Although the word "praise" was scribbled on that little paper, I just could not do it. Praising Him with a thankful heart seemed impossible. I had memorized the words of the apostle Paul in 1 Thessalonians 5:18, *"In everything give thanks"* (NKJV). To transition from memorization to practice was easier said than done. I knew that I had to do it, but I couldn't…not yet!

Conviction settled into my soul and I knew that if I did not thank God for "everything" I would be a disobedient follower. To be a fully devoted follower of Jesus is to follow in obedience, including "thanksgiving in everything."

It was the eve of our departure for Quito; we were staying with friends in the Canal Zone. The children were asleep. I was alone, and it was almost midnight. I had to verbalize my words of thanksgiving, not just think the thoughts in my head. In the darkness of that guest room, I said, "Lord, I do not understand. I know your ways are not my ways, and your thoughts are higher than mine. So even though I do not understand, I know you are my Sovereign Lord and I thank you for all that you have taken away." It was tough, but Jesus gave me the grace to praise. Christ is Sovereign and He is Lord.

Following in obedience is my only responsibility.

The Blessing of Encouragement through Letters Received

Among the many letters received was one from my mom when she arrived back in Canada. Her letter, shared with many, is a summary of her observations while in Panama. Mom was overwhelmed with the demonstration of love poured out during our time of crisis. She wrote,

> Having had a little glimpse of Panama under very trying circumstances, it was difficult to form definite ideas and opinions. It is a land of great natural beauty. The people are very affectionate, extremely kind, and how we did wish we could communicate with them! However, it is amazing how, in many ways, one can communicate.
>
> We met many new Christians, steadfast in their faith and full of the joy of the Lord. As these dear people came to call on Jean and the children, their love was so warm and evident. From morning until night, numbers from far and near kept coming every day. Seldom did they leave without forming a circle, holding hands and praying. Their extreme kindness and hospitality was just overwhelming—they literally supplied our every need. They brought lovely hot meals, salads, baking, deserts, fruit, lunches, cold drinks and ice. They supplied cars and drivers; their kindness knew no bounds. I've never witnessed such loving concern. Words just cannot describe it all. The great love these people had for Jean, Gil and the children was beyond telling. You just had to see and feel it.
>
> During our stay we visited "The Farm" where the missionary children attend school. I met Miss Friesen, their teacher; Daryl and Shari, their general helpers; and I saw Auntie Ruth in action, supplying everyone's needs and seeing to their comfort. Ruth is a marvel—keeps everything organized and on time. Uncle Gordon was always there, ready and willing for whatever needed his attention. This tragedy has been a real blow to the entire group of missionaries.
>
> Mrs. Reimer and I attended one of the Women's Bible study groups that Jean led, and believe me, that was really something!

Those women are alive and alert, had their Scripture portions studied and prepared. Their discussion and prayer times were so wonderful.

We also attended a Christian Women's luncheon, where Mrs. J. Allen Blair was the speaker. We met so many wonderful people. A young woman seated beside me said, "I just know you are Jean's mom. I'd like to tell you what Gil and Jean have meant to my husband and I. We have seven children. We were just like heathen, but now, through their witness and testimony and instruction, we gave our hearts to the Lord and our home is like heaven now."

I met the missionaries that we had learned to know only through letters but now got to meet personally—David and Martha, Al and Tish, Ventura and Mary, Linda and Helen. I was hearing bits and pieces of their work and learning of victories won. Panama is a little piece of God's handiwork and beauty, but the transformed lives of many who have personally come to know Him was marvelous.

Do pray especially for those who have answered God's call and are faithfully serving there. I have thought, how wonderful it would be if we could all take a holiday under normal conditions. Instead of going to California or Florida or wherever, we could visit some mission field to see first hand what it means to be a missionary, their conditions, the people and many other factors of a missionary life."

Mom concluded her letter by requesting prayer for us. She wrote, "Please continue to remember Jean, Glen, Betti Lou, Cliff and Diana. They need our prayer support now more than ever before."

During those first weeks in Quito, after the children left for school I continued to read the letters and sympathy cards that arrived daily. I read and I cried! I cried and I read. More than once, I would arrive for lunch at the guest house with puffy eyes! We received some seven hundred letters tucked inside envelopes with stamps from all over the world!

Several wrote, "We do not know you, and you don't know us. When one suffers in the body of Christ, we all suffer." Others wrote of the impact that Gil had on their lives. During our few months in Ecuador, plans were made to eat our weekday noon and evening meals in the GMU guest house, just down the street from our apartment. Sundays could have been lonely, but they weren't. We were invited out to lunch every Sunday morning after worship service. Following the evening church service, the children and I never went back alone to our one-room apartment on the second floor. We were loved, pampered and blessed beyond measure.

Living in Quito, Ecuador was a new experience for all of us. We enjoyed the "forever spring-like" weather high in the Andes Mountains. The love of those "in the neighborhood" was evident on a daily basis. I doubt if I will ever get over the incredible blessing and comfort received from those right around us. Each day, even with a tearstained face, I had reason to celebrate the goodness of God.

The pastor at the International Church became our pastor. Marge Saint VanderPuy and Barbara Youdarian blessed me with wisdom, as they had been down my road before, being the widows of two of the five missionary men speared to death by the Waodani tribe.

Have I mentioned how wonderful it is to belong to the family of God?

Roses and a Glass of Spilled Water

Then came the morning I shall never forget. As usual I got up before the children, showered and prepared for the day. The bathroom was adequate, but too small to dress after our showers. Right outside the bathroom door, we placed our fresh clean clothes on a highboy dresser so they were easily accessible and within arm's reach.

The day before, a newly acquired friend from the American Embassy had sent us a dozen roses. The crystal vase filled with beautiful roses was placed on top and center of the highboy. On the left side were my clean clothes. On the right side was a pile of 700 recently written prayer letters just back from the printers, 700 envelopes and 700 Ecuadorian stamps.

ANYWHERE, ANYTIME, ANY COST

When I finished showering, I slightly opened the door and reached out to get my clothes, only to discover that they were rather damp. While I had been in the bathroom, Glen had thrown his pajama top at his little sister and missed! It hit the roses and the rest of the story needs no explanation.

Things were damp. We put 700 stamps on 700 envelopes without having to lick even one. I stormed at my kids—I don't remember all that I said, but they were not words of encouragement. That morning when Glen and Betti Lou left for the Alliance Academy, their Irish mom was mad. I hugged them, but loving words were absent.

They left and I was left alone, well, not quite! The presence of God and the voice of the Holy Spirit were very real. He spoke loudly into my heart and I heard Him say, "Jean, you have just come through the most horrific and most difficult experience of your life. You praised Me, you thanked Me for giving you My peace, I assured you of My presence. You experienced the grace that I lavished on you. You experienced My enablement and empowerment. Now, over a simple glass of spilled water, you have totally lost it!"

As you can imagine, when Glen and Betti Lou came home at noon for lunch, I embraced them and held them close and apologized. I could have blamed the whole incident on the fact that I am one hundred percent Irish. The truth was I was functioning and reacting in the flesh and not drawing on the resources available to me in Christ Jesus.

And yes, as we go through life, perhaps few will lose a loved one by a horrendous stabbing, but everyone of us will have a glass of spilled water!

Unexpected Location Change

Three Months Translate into One Year

MY MINISTRY DESIGNATION HAD BEEN CHANGED FROM CHURCH PLANTING IN PANAMA City to a varied ministry in Quito. The Alliance Academy in Quito had replaced Elim Academy in Panama. And now, it was time to leave for three months in Canada. The exit date was on cue, but the departure city had changed. Surely these were enough changes. Could there possibly be any more? I thought not. We planned to be back!

Before I left Quito, in response to the 700 letters received, I wrote a news update prayer letter to send to each one who had written. The following were excerpts . . .

> We have just passed through experiences outlined by God . . . I dare not ask "Why, Lord?" Faith does not ask but accepts that His ways are higher than our ways and His thoughts higher than our thoughts ... so much higher!
>
> Yes, there have been tears. We miss our beloved Gil very much. But as Betti Lou said last night: "My daddy was just perfect, but he wouldn't want to come back to this wicked world, would he?" Many have written that Gil packed more into his thirty-six years than many do in seventy!
>
> Someone said, "God takes care of the span of our lives, but it is up to us to take care of the depth." For nearly thirteen years, God gave me the joy of sharing life with an enthusiastic Christian, wonderful husband and father.

God's grace is proving sufficient and daily He gives His peace, strength, His comfort and His joy. Doctrine known for so long is now being translated into experience. I am learning the reality of 1 Peter 2:24—His wounds heal ours.

You've been so special as you have showered us with so much love and prayer. Our desire is that God will lead us "through the valley and out . . . not somehow, but triumphantly."

The letters were mailed, the tickets purchased, suitcases packed and we were ready to fly to Canada. This time it would be different. It would be the first time arriving without our Gil.

Within a few days our plane touched down at the Winnipeg Airport. It was harder than we anticipated, as it was the first time friends and family were welcoming just three, not four, of us.

We were now home with our parents and siblings! After a few days being loved by Gil's parents and family in Steinbach, Manitoba, and a day's drive to Meyronne, Saskatchewan, I was back in the kitchen where I grew up. To say that it was wonderful to be embraced by our families and close friends is an understatement. Time was of essence; every day was intentionally planned, as in three months a return flight to Quito was scheduled.

It was during this short visit with my folks that we made a quick trip to the Briercrest Bible College campus at Caronport, Saskatchewan. It was intended to be just a quick "Hello" and "Thanks for all your prayers." One brief greeting turned into a serious and unexpected invitation.

During our visit on campus with Dr. Henry Hildebrand, founder and president of Briercrest College, he blessed us with his wise counsel. Although we had gone through a difficult and traumatic crisis, we believed we had transitioned well. I assume the deep circles underlining our eyes told more than I thought. Dr. Hildebrand wisely suggested that we needed time to recover from the trauma all three of us had experienced. Furthermore, Dr. Hildebrand was so sure of this, that he put a vacant lot for a mobile home "on hold." He had also made inquires into possible employment. It did not take long to understand that the wisdom of Dr. Hildebrand was advice we would do well to heed. As we drove the couple of hours back to my farm home, our thoughts went wild with the unexpected possible changes before us.

Anywhere? As I scribbled my signature on that small card, was I really trusting God with my zip code, even though the new *postal* code would be SOH OSO?

Arriving back on the farm, we talked a mile a minute retelling the conversation that had concluded a few hours earlier. My folks were thrilled with the thought of their grandchildren living only a couple of hours down the highway. My parents-in-law were joyous. They were well acquainted with Briercrest, the alma mater of two of their daughters, Vange and Noreen, and son-in-law Monroe.

But there was a wedding to attend in Steinbach, Manitoba, before I began work at Briercrest and the children began classes. I'll let my sister-in-law Noreen tell it as it happened:

A few years earlier during a furlough Gil and I sang together, sometimes accompanied by a pianist in our church, a tall good-looking single guy. Gil and I shared a similar thought—the man on the piano bench was not a bad catch! Even though Gil had always told me it was my duty to stay single so I could take care of our parents in their old age, he seemed to think this might be okay.

In the fall of 1973, Gil wrote, "There is an overlap of two weeks when both Cliff and Diana and we are going to be home on furlough; make sure something significant happens." I wrote on my friends' calendar on August 31, "Noreen's wedding"—in faith, no man in sight.

After Gil's death I got a letter of sympathy from the tall good-looking pianist, who had also lost a brother and sister-in-law. That was the beginning. The wedding happened on August 30, 1974. Gil was not there, but having orchestrated it with God, he was probably looking on in delight.

Joyously, Gil had orchestrated the details of his sister's wedding identifying the groom and determining the date. My emotions were plainly described by the tears I fought as I witnessed Ernie and Noreen's beautiful wedding . . . alone.

God gave assurance and peace that Briercrest was His plan for the next year. A phone call secured the mobile home lot that had been "on hold." Now, all was about to change. There would not be a return flight to Quito as planned.

Anywhere? . . . has ramifications.

This change of plans meant a mobile home needed to be found and bought. A mobile home would cost thousands of dollars—thousands I did not have. As we had lived from one remittance to another, when Gil had transferred to his home in heaven, we did not have much in our bank account. How would God possibly provide? Could I trust Him with this one?

Before Gil and I returned to Panama the last time, a close friend representing an insurance company urged Gil to take out life insurance. He kept urging. Gil kept resisting. Gil was convinced that, at our young age, we certainly did not need life insurance! Moreover, our missionary budget did not include sufficient for monthly insurance premiums. "Thanks, but no thanks," was our final answer. However, Fred was so convinced that Gil needed a life insurance policy that he gave a gracious gift of money to our mission organization to be deposited to our account.

Just two years later, Gil was gone. Our friend from the insurance company was in total disbelief as he saw the death notice in his city paper. Unbelievable!

His death certificate had been sent to the insurance company and soon the cheque would be in the mail. However, Fred and Muriel decided to drive eight hours to personally deliver it. The amount of that insurance cheque was just what was needed for a large down payment on a mobile home!

After personally delivering the cheque, Fred asked permission for he and Muriel to sing Andre Crouch's recent song, "Through It All."

They sang. I wept. It was true. I was in the process of learning to trust through it all.

God had done it again! Two years before, He had orchestrated all the details. There was money for a mobile home, without my even knowing that I would need one.

JESUS. Still growing in amazement!

Anywhere? I relinquished my zip code to Him and God in His faithfulness provided one more time.

All within short seven months, our move took us from a spacious high-rise condo in Panama City to a one room apartment in Quito, Ecuador, to a mobile home on a Canadian prairie college campus!

God beautifully provided a new two-bedroom mobile home with a lovely kitchen, dining room and large living room, which became the first home we owned. I bought it in Calgary, Canada's rodeo city, and had it moved down the TransCanada highway to the college campus in Caronport, located near the famous large metric moose outside of Moose Jaw, Saskatchewan.

The generous help and assistance of many close friends and family made the move less complicated than anticipated. However, becoming accustomed to life on a prairie college campus had its challenges.

Our first meal in our brand new dining room is one never to be forgotten. The table was set for three rather than four. Someone very precious and cherished was missing. There were no words, no appetite, only tears. We tried to eat, but we couldn't. Establishing a new home without our beloved Gil was more difficult than we could ever have imagined.

Grieving did not end, and tears did continue, especially during those times when I was alone. It took its toll on the children as well.

Glen recalls, "I remember having nightmares most nights, where communists would come to our door in the night and take away Mom and Betts from me."

Betti Lou remembers, "Because I never saw my daddy in the coffin, I couldn't believe that he was really gone forever. I remember going to bed most nights worried that if somehow Daddy was still alive, he would never be able to find us since we had moved twice since Panama— to Ecuador and Canada. I would lay awake at night wondering how he would ever find us."

While still in the initial stages of adjustment, I awoke just past midnight to hear the cries of my ten-year-old, Glen. I entered his small bedroom and within minutes discovered the reason for his tears. When he told me that it was all my fault, I was puzzled to say the least. He continued, "Mom, why don't you read the Bible?" I assured him that I was regularly reading the Bible. Amid sobs, his response was, "Then, why don't you obey it?" I just did not understand where he was going with all this. He then explained, "Mommy, the Bible says that God disciplines those whom He loves. Since Dad died, you haven't spanked me once."

I wasn't ready for this answer but explained that he had not needed a spanking, trying to assure him that my love for him had absolutely not changed and I loved him with all my heart. Then I recalled that for some time Glen, as a young boy, had been reading a chapter from Proverbs each day, going through Proverbs once every month. No doubt he had spent time pondering the meaning of Proverbs 13:24 and had come to what he thought was an obvious conclusion.

The months continued and the routine of classes and work became the new norm. However, one late afternoon while the children were out, three of us met, but not the usual three. It was just "me, myself and I!" We had a "self-soul" talk. As I thought about the future, I knew that I had two choices before me. I could sit on my sofa every day and have a pity party, or I could get off the sofa to bless and encourage others. A choice had to be made. I chose the latter.

Living on a student campus, we were surrounded by hundreds of students—elementary, high school and college students. It wasn't long before our small mobile home overflowed and opportunities abounded. I had grieved, and tears at times still flowed, but in the context of grief I was learning to reach out to others who might also have holes hidden in their hearts.

Opportunities to minister in churches were many. The balancing act of family and ministry was difficult, and I grappled with how to manage both. This was as really a tough one! I did say "Yes" to several speaking invitations. There were also times when those who extended the invitation could not understand the word "No." On one occasion I received an interesting phone call. A committee had decided to invite me to be their keynote speaker at an upcoming conference. Following their decision, the director called to invite me but would not take "No" for an answer! Lacking finesse, she abruptly asked, "Why don't you start practicing the grace you talk about?" then hung up.

All of this had an impact on all three of us. As Glen grappled with our situation, he summarized, "Mom had evening and summer ministries, and this sometimes made me feel that I'd lost a mom as well as a dad. However, I never resented the ministry that God gave to Mom. It was very key in my life that Mom was not bitter against God for allowing Dad to be killed. As a result, I remember feeling loss and pain in many different ways, but I do not remember ever feeling bitterness against God. I do remember feeling His strong presence with us throughout this time."

My working days at Briercrest began in the library. It was a new experience. I love books and people. But before too many months had passed, it became evident to some that I belonged in the classroom not a library. Was I really that loud?

The very possibility of college teaching never entered my mind! College classrooms would be totally out of my comfort zone! Why would I even entertain such a wild idea? For if that were to happen, I would have to upgrade my education. What a scary thought! I was daily hearing the groans of students seated in their library carrels, their minds engaged in assignments, papers and exams. As a new widow with children, why would I even want to go down that road?

Was there not another option? Couldn't I just return to Ecuador?

As the months crept by that first year working in the library, many advised me to return to the classroom, get the B. A. in Biblical Studies and then consider a teaching position. My supervisor was one, among others, who strongly recommended that I prepare for the classroom. To appease those who were urging me to complete my degree, I made an appointment with the college registrar to find out how many hours I lacked for a Bachelor of Arts degree. Later that week and just five minutes before the noon lunch break, I walked down to the registrar's office to get the results. Before I left for lunch, I shared the registrar's report with the librarian, my supervisor.

Within one hour of discovering how much time I would need to get a B. A. and informing the librarian, I was replaced. All within one hour! The thought of being the provider without an income and becoming a student was overwhelming! Could I trust God with this one too? Was it really becoming evident that I would not be returning to Latin America? So many changes in less than twelve months!

The librarian who replaced me within one hour also replaced my fears with the assurance of his help, including tutoring me in my first course. His offer was the answer to a desperate cry for help as I delved into the books, classes and assignments. But really, what had I committed to? At forty, I was returning to the classroom to become a full time student again.

While I am on the topic of further education, I am going to jump ahead and share how God blessed me with friends who helped me make academic choices that otherwise would have been ignored.

Personal goals and plans were to finish a B. A. in Biblical Studies with no thought of continuing on to further studies. If it had not been for Dr. Paul Magnus who urged, inspired and encouraged me to continue studies, I would not have reentered the classroom as a student.

His helpful assistance enabled me to enroll in Grace Theological Seminary in Winona Lake, Indiana, to complete a Master's degree. The modular courses were offered during the four summer months, making it possible for our family to move there. God blessed us with Diane, who became "our governess" for the summer months. Diane was part of our family and we loved her dearly. What joy to spend two wonderful invigorating summers together in Indiana!

I assumed continuing education was now a closed topic. However, Dr. Magnus motivated me to think differently and suggested I pray about a Doctor of Missiology degree. With his encouragement and help, I applied to Trinity International University in Deerfield, Illinois.

The courses and class discussions were stimulating and I loved learning. It was the course requirements and assignments that caused a few tears and moments of desperation.

Because all the classes were in the modular format, I was able to take my time and fit in courses when possible. My priority was my family, so going at a slow pace allowed for time both as a homemaker and a student. Learning under the instruction of godly skilled professors was amazing and pure joy. I am grateful to Dr. Magnus and my colleagues for their wise counsel in the decisions and choices I faced.

From the Library to the Classroom . . .

During the next year there were three students in our home rather than two! Glen was in Grade Six, Betti Lou in Grade Four and Mom, a freshman in college!

The first college course I registered for was Apologetics with Dr. Henry Budd, who was a great teacher and friend but whose lectures were "over my head." He referred to early philosophers such as Soren Kierkegard, Immanuel Kant, Friederich Nietzche and Jean-Paul Sartre as if they were household names. Was I the only one in the class who was clueless? From noting the interaction in class discussion, the answer to that question was a definite "yes!" When the course modular was completed, Dr. Budd asked me why I did not participate and contribute to the class discussions. I had just been out of academic circulation too long!

Then there was the Greek class that I signed up for. I loved the challenge but there were not enough hours in the day for the many required hours of study, so I decided to bail out. The attempt was unsuccessful. Why did I ever register for a Greek class?

However, being a student as a widow with young children definitely had its perks. Before I wrote any of the many Greek exams, Glen or Betti Lou would suggest that we go to the living room, hold hands and form a circle while one would pray that Mom would pass her Greek exam. Then we would all wait for the results. When the grades were posted, their first question always was, "Mom, what did we get on the exam?" Can't beat that for teamwork!

Al, the librarian, continued being a great encourager as he offered to tutor me in one of the first courses which was Methods of Bible Study. I loved the course! As Al tutored me in Methods of Bible Study, I tried to figure out how I had spent nearly twenty years as a missionary without these foundational principles for personally discovering Truth.

From a Mobile Home to an Apartment, from a Student to a Teacher...

Over two years, the mobile home became smaller as the children became older. One apartment of an apartment block was available to rent, so we decided to make the move. Unlike the mobile home, it was not furnished. I will be forever grateful for family and friends who blessed us when help and furniture was needed. Local Manitoba businessmen helped with the needed furniture, and family members and friends graciously offered to help. It was a day's journey in the cold of a January prairie winter, but Monroe and Vange, Ernie and Ardyth loaded, drove and helped set up furniture in incredibly cold weather, making a "house" our new "home."

After one year as a student, life changed and I switched places in the classroom from in front of to behind the podium. Methods of Bible Study, Ephesians and Speech were the first courses assigned. Hours of preparation were required daily and at times preparation continued into the night.

My passion for the classroom grew as I discovered that I could walk into a classroom weary and leave invigorated. Students energized me. Life surrounded by hundreds of students was a marvelous plan that only God could put together.

God used students to refine and challenge my own spiritual walk in obedience. Doug was one of those students. He was only weeks old in Jesus when he came to Briercrest and enrolled in my class on Ephesians. Before my very eyes, I saw him grow spiritually. Midway through the semester, I asked him, "Doug, you have grown so much in Christ; how is this happening?"

He replied, "Well, Mrs. Reimer, I just read and obey, read and obey, read and obey. I didn't know there was an option." A profound and foundational truth that somehow is easy to miss!

Students continued to encourage me in many and diverse ways. I vividly recall one morning in particular. My lecture had concluded and the class was over when three young freshmen men came up to the podium and asked, "Who do you hang out with?" I asked them what they had in mind, to which they responded, "Well, we just want to hang out with you. May we?"

Hanging out with students became my absolute delight!

Not every day was a "sunshine in my soul" kind of day, as there were also days when I was weary in body, soul and spirit. I recall one such day. Despondency hovered over me as I trudged down Centre Street to my office. As I walked, I prayed, asking God to manifest the assurance of His understanding love by just having someone give me a smile.

I imagined the answer to my brief prayer would be a smile offered by someone in the halls of the Administration Building. However, it didn't happen that way. While seated at my desk, a student came by my office door and, with his nose pressed against my door window, stopped long enough to give me the biggest Cheshire grin ever imagined, leaving behind a loving smudge. What a wonderful reminder of my God who understands and uplifts His weary child.

Anywhere? It became so evident that it was God writing the story!

The suggested one year on a college campus turned into twenty-six! He had a plan and orchestrated every step and provided for every need. As I reflect on the years spent on this college campus, my mind goes back to the faculty who built into my life and I thank God for each one.

I am grateful for the professor who urged me to be a woman of the Word. I thank God for the one who believed in me, stretching me with assignments impossible to accomplish apart from God. I thank God for the professor who was there for our family, one whom I could call on at any hour of the morning or night knowing he would be there to shepherd us through our hurts. I thank God for each of my fellow faculty members, whose office doors would always be open to dialog, get advice or just chat. Faculty, staff and students touched our lives in countless ways.

The Faculty and Staff Bible Study and Prayer Meeting held each Wednesday evening was one of the best things happening on campus! There were times when I arrived weary but left energized and strengthened by the faithful exposition of the WORD taught by our president and other professors.

In twenty-four years, I had as many faculty assistants and teaching interns as years. Each one was unique, loved and indispensable. They read and graded literally hundreds and hundreds of assignments. I would

143

like to think that performing their student work in a missions focused office had an impact on their future ministry locations. Today, they are scattered across the globe, having served or are serving in countries such as Tanzania, Mongolia, Uganda, Siberia, South and North Africa, Mali Republic, Ghana, Japan, Peru, Bolivia, France, Austria and Portugal. Others have remained in North America, becoming professional and successful leaders in their fields of employment and calling. My heart overflows with gratitude for each one. They have blessed, inspired, encouraged, and yes, many times put a smile on my face and made me laugh. Now, years later, as our paths cross, they are still bringing an enormous smile of gratitude.

Ministry Opportunities Outside the Classroom ....

On the day I yielded everything to His Lordship, there was no way I could even imagine the ministry opportunities He had prepared or the doors that would open.

Serving as the Faculty Advisor for the Student Missions Fellowship was such an unexpected privilege. SMF gave me the opportunity to see up close the global hearts of young adults. Each week they organized and attended weekly mission prayer bands. They led Thursday morning missions focused chapel programs that were informative, inspirational and challenging. A highlight was the annual conference for SMF leaders representing many Bible colleges across the Canadian prairies.

Missionary kids, also known as Third Culture Kids (TCK's) or Global Nomads, are unique and very special. What a joy to be their Faculty Advisor! They have traveled around the world, been in countless airports, have crossed many cultures, learned languages and are blessed with a worldview and God-view so much bigger than those of their contemporaries. Hearing the MK's pray for missions was so enriching, as they prayed with so much insight and wisdom.

From my perspective, Third Culture Kids are wonderful. Therefore, I have my own personal and unique philosophy which is, "If you can't be one, make one."

It was the beginning of another school year. Classes had ended for the day and I was called to the office of the Academic Dean. His vision

144

was to see a musical group that would minister in churches, providing an emphasis on missions in drama and song. He asked me to organize and lead such a team. The other ministry teams had already been chosen, so it would be a challenge, if not impossible, to find potential members. I hesitated. "If you do not do it, I have someone else in mind," he explained. Selfish as I am, I did not want someone else to get the blessing, so I agreed to organize a Missions Musical Team.

Where would I begin? Authenticity required that each member be surrendered to the Lordship of Christ, willing to go anywhere in the world for Him. God provided a musical octet and a pianist. We called ourselves "Mandate." We ministered in churches throughout the school year and toured each summer across Canada and the USA. What a privilege of leading and ministering with young adults committed to doing His will—anywhere, anytime, at any cost.

While in my office one morning, I received a phone call, inviting me to organize and initiate the first Evangelical Missiological Society in Western Canada. I hesitated but accepted. The challenge was huge, so having surrounded myself with a visionary team, we trusted God for wisdom. The next year the first annual conference of EMS Western Canada began on the campus of Prairie Bible College. Dr. David Hesselgrave, a beloved professor at Trinity International University, offered to be our first keynote speaker. God gave a successful beginning, and annual EMS conferences continue to enrich Christian leaders.

"Jean, why don't you take a male quartet to Panama for a summer ministry?" was a question posed by Dr. David, a fellow faculty member. That was all I needed to spark a vision of leading a short-term team. It would be my first visit back to Panama as a widow with the children. Leading a missions team was a new experience, but the idea invigorated me. I also knew that if a team was to be effective, it must be adequately equipped.

I was aware of a male quartet already formed on campus. It only took an invitation. The quartet and their pianist were ready for the challenge. Later, a gifted soloist, a chalk artist and three others asked to go. A team was formed, numbering thirteen in total, including my children and myself. We were "His Instruments."

What would "adequately prepared" look like? Knowing that Jesus said, *"For without Me you can do nothing"* (John 15:5, NKJV), we were totally dependent upon Him. Weekly prayer meetings and language classes began in January for a June departure. In orchestrating all the details, God led a missionary couple from Argentina to Briercrest. They devoted hours to teaching Spanish to the team members. Before we flew to Panama, the quartet had learned and committed to memory the lyrics of eleven quartet numbers in Spanish. The soloist had learned and memorized all her solos in Spanish. Each of the members had prepared their testimonies in Spanish.

While in Panama for six weeks, His Instruments presented Canadian Cultural Programs in high schools during the day and participated in the Evangelistic Tent Meetings at night. They sang, gave their testimonies, did chalk art and shared their stories under that huge tent. Aaron, a former Panama missionary, a Nicaraguan evangelist, a missionary cook, a bus driver and thirteen Canadians formed our team.

To say that I was totally at ease to be back in Panama following Gil's murder would have been an understatement. For the most part, I was relaxed. However, one July night while eating the evening meal at a hotel, I realized that there were several men staring in our direction. I knew they were not Panamanians. I was bothered by their unending stares and chatter, experiencing a real sense that all was not well in the hotel that night.

Upon our arrival back in Canada, a friend asked, "While you were in Panama, what happened on one specific night in July?" She explained that God had awakened her in the night to pray for me. She said, "I prayed, and God continued to awaken me until I stayed up all night to pray for your safety. Were you in trouble?" I thank God for friends who will pray, all night if needed. I was grateful for His watchful care. He knows who to awaken in the night to pray. God had put a hedge of protection about the children and me. He heard, when a friend prayed—all night!

God gave me the joy of serving on and off of a college campus, in and out of a college classroom and beyond the Missions Faculty office! When I think about it, I wonder why, at times, I was so hesitant to walk through open doors. In every one of the ministry opportunities, God gave me a front row seat of seeing Him direct, provide, equip and lavish His grace.

During my years on campus, there were many opportunities to practice hospitality and I wonder how many times I served "angels unaware." One day a mission director and his wife were visiting the campus representing their mission organization. I didn't know them well but God prompted my heart to invite them home to dinner. All I had were five processed chicken pot pies in my freezer that I had bought for just eighty-five cents each.

Throughout the day I argued with myself, "Pot pies are okay for us, but certainly not for the director of a mission society and his wife." As God the Holy Spirit quietly urged me to invite them to dinner, I swallowed my pride and submitted to His prompting.

We had finished our dinner of chicken pot pies and salad and had enjoyed a wonderful time of fellowship. Just before our friends left that evening, the director's wife commented, "Thank you so much for inviting us to your home tonight. Today I prayed that we would not have to eat in the college dining hall. Today is my husband's birthday and I wanted it to be special for him. So, I asked God to have someone invite us to their home." Wow! Because of my desire to impress rather than bless, I almost missed the joy of obedience.

To adequately summarize the blessings of twenty-six years would be impossible. How does one fully describe, in a paragraph or two, God's mercies that were new every morning? Impossible. I pray that the stories recounted have given you just a small glimpse into His awesome grace and faithfulness during those many years on a college campus.

Following twenty-four years as a college professor, God led us to serve again with GMU, now AVANT Ministries. In a three-year assignment, I served as Assistant to the President for International Training at their international headquarters in Kansas City, Missouri. In this role, I helped develop training programs for missionaries in all phases of ministry. They were three years of incredible blessings, wonderful new friendships, ministry opportunities and challenges blended into one.

While in Kansas City, I celebrated my birthday and sixty-five years of God's goodness. The golden age had arrived for senior perks and pension. From Kansas City we moved to Calgary, Alberta, at the foothills of the Canadian Rockies and the home of the Calgary Stampede, the biggest outdoor rodeo in the world.

Retirement had begun.

At the outset of retirement, I boarded a flight in Calgary for Abbotsford, BC. What happened next occurred upon landing at the Abbotsford International Airport.

Lorne, the Canadian Director for TEAM, and I were on the same flight headed to Missions Fest Vancouver. While walking to the terminal we chatted. The question was, "What is happening in missions?" Trying to answer that question was the beginning of many talks, dialogues and meetings at Ricky's restaurant on Country Hills Boulevard in Calgary. We summarized the current Canadian scene and envisioned what could yet happen for God's glory.

We soon discovered that our vision of a one-year missions equipping program for cross-cultural ministries was shared by other mission leaders, college professors and church leaders. We envisioned a program in partnership with mission agencies, local churches and Bible colleges.

All we had was a vision and an idea. We had no director, no professors, no students, no classrooms and no money. But we had faith to believe that this venture was placed in our hearts by God. We prayed, planned and programmed for three years. Then, with only three students, CrossTraining Global began.

Now eight years later, we are celebrating what God alone could do. He provided the director, the professors, the students, classrooms and finances. Today, we thank God for forty countries where fifty-five CTG graduates have completed their internships. All are now serving either as long term overseas global workers or as missionary appointees, or in church ministries. Others are still pursuing a cross-cultural ministry, but all with a heart for the world.

Nothing could have happened without our partnerships with twenty-seven mission agencies, four Bible colleges, Calgary churches—

including nineteen local ethnic churches providing student practicums and mentorships—outstanding mission professors and the commitment and vision of our directors.

Now CTG has transferred to Toronto, the largest cosmopolitan city in the world. This is really reason to celebrate!

Retirement . . .

What joy was mine when I received a call from Millar College of the Bible in Saskatchewan! They extended an invitation to teach Mission Trends and Practices, a modular missions course, to their fourth year students. I can't remember saying, "I'll pray about it." I was just excited with the opportunity! I am now in my sixth year as adjunct faculty at Millar College, having added another one-week modular course called Introduction to Missions. How God has blessed me as I have seen first hand what God is doing in a small Bible college on the Saskatchewan prairies!

Anytime? Age doesn't count when God has a plan!

Family Alterations

Grateful to Be Close to Parents in Their Senior Years

AFTER YEARS SEPARATED GEOGRAPHICALLY BY THOUSANDS OF MILES, LIFE BACK in Canada gave the opportunity to be within driving distance of our families. What joy to be near my parents and parents-in-law during their aging years!

I have friends who would say that I have an addiction to buying greeting cards. It was a winter morning on the prairies, while in Moose Jaw I browsed in the greeting card section in Eaton's Department Store. One card caught my eye. It was a Thank-You card with words that perfectly expressed gratitude to my parents for their faithful support and blessing us in countless ways.

I bought it, threw it on my office desk at home, then forgot it . . . until one Friday noon hour. I was home for a quick lunch when the Holy Spirit prompted me pick up that card, write an additional few lines, address the envelope and drop it in the mailbox on my way back to class. Although I was in a hurry and time was limited during the noon hour that Friday, I did it.

The next day my card arrived in the mail. It was early afternoon when Dad and Mom received and read my Thank-You note. At five o'clock that evening, without any warning, my dad took a massive heart attack and died. Busyness could have easily deterred me from God's purposes, and I would have missed saying a final "thank you" to my dad. I will never cease to be amazed that the Holy Spirit quietly urged and prompted me, because . . .

God had a plan for my Dad on Saturday!

Dad's threefold desire was to die on the farm, with his boots on and helping someone. God granted all three of his requests. Dad was a generous giver, and even before death, he made Mom promise that she would buy the cheapest casket, to make more money available for missions.

My mom lived by herself in a small cottage an hour away but spent many winters with us. Mom and Opal, our next door neighbor, became close friends. Even though both were advanced in age, they enjoyed more than one adventurous trip together. Mom's days were filled with severe pain from bone cancer, but she lived each day with purpose and definite goals to reach before bedtime.

Her final three months were spent in the hospital. My brothers, twin sister, a friend Ruth and I took turns staying with her around the clock as she was heaven bound. What a privilege to be at her side just moments before her earthly tent folded and she took flight to heaven!

Mom and Dad Reimer were living in Steinbach, Manitoba, spending their final years in a Nursing Home. Mom arrived in heaven seven years before Dad. I can't imagine their joy of being in the very presence of God and being reunited with Gil!

Our parents went to heaven without ever learning the motive of Gil's death. In the years that followed, we were all still speculating a possible motive. Now in heaven, our parents no longer need to wonder and speculate, they know all the details and so much more. They have the answers to some of the questions that on earth are still being asked. No doubt they have spent hours with Gil. I wonder if he has related the dreadful circumstances of those horrifying last hours, or are the details of that eventful night insignificant in comparison to being in the very presence of our Lord?

I thank God for loving parents and parents-in-law. What a blessing to be in Canada during their final years and to be able to attend and participate in their funerals. We loved them dearly. Each one had such an integral part in our lives and ministry as they prayed, encouraged, shared and gave of themselves sacrificially.

Wedding Bells in the Chapel

During the years of widowhood, I experienced all the blessings that God promises for widows, as revealed in His Word. Isaiah 54 was especially meaningful. We had great friends who loved to help. "Yentas" were plentiful. One evening Lorraine attended a conference where I was the keynote speaker. Lorraine and her husband were friends of widower, Alton Barsness, and on their first opportunity to meet, she mentioned my name to him.

It was just another Caronport High School graduation, but this one had unexpected personal ramifications. Duane Barsness was among many high school graduates. His proud father, Alton, and sisters, Berva and Carol, were there to celebrate this milestone. Berva introduced me to her father, who had been a widower for fifteen years. Several had talked to Alton about a widow, a college teacher at Caronport. Interesting how "Fiddler on the Roof" had only one yenta, but they seemed to abound on the Canadian prairies! It did not take long for us to sense God's leading and provision. While I was studying at Grace Seminary in Winona Lake, Indiana, that summer, we were engaged in the home of Dr. John C. and Norma Whitcome. In the fall, wedding bells rang in the chapel on Briercrest campus.

Claire and Ruth and I received our diplomas in the same graduating class many years ago at Briercrest. They moved to Pennsylvania and I moved to Panama. Years later, while the Greiner Family Singers were on campus, mutual friends invited the Greiner family and the Reimer trio to join them for lunch. It was during lunch that Bevan noticed Betts for the first time; she was just fifteen. Bevan waited. Five years later on March 30, 1986, Betts and Bevan were married and wedding bells rang again in the chapel on the Briercrest campus.

Two years following our arrival at Briercrest, we were getting ready for church one Sunday morning. I struggled as I helped Glen with his tie. I became frustrated with not being able to help. He became frustrated with me not knowing how. We needed help, so we called George who, with his family, lived on the other side of the wall in our apartment block. Little did we imagine that the neighbor who would teach him how to knot a tie would later become his father-in-law! On December 9,

1989, Glen married George and Louise's daughter and they committed their lives to each other. Wedding bells rang a third time in the chapel on the Briercrest campus.

International Ministry Opportunities

Anywhere?

Airports and Customs

WE HAD TWENTY-SIX YEARS ON A COLLEGE CAMPUS AND THREE YEARS SERVING at AVANT Mission Headquarters, then God graciously gave me opportunities to minister internationally in more than fifteen countries, in Africa, Asia, Europe and Central and South America. God provided opportunities to see firsthand what He was doing in and through men and women dedicated to Him. Many hours have been spent in airports, waiting in customs lines and going through the screening process before takeoff. There are many airport stories, but one in particular illustrates the goodness and miraculous ways of God.

A friend and I were in the Beijing Airport, en route to Mongolia. My son, who was a teacher there, invited me to spend a couple of weeks with him. At his request we were taking two hockey duffle bags filled with food. Each duffle bag had layers and layers of food in ziplock plastic bags. He asked if I would bring an axe, which they needed to chop wood for the wood stove inside their Mongolian gher. I bought and stuffed that axe carefully in the middle of my duffle bag surrounded and encompassed by plastic ziplock bags.

I was okay with the idea of having an axe in my luggage until I saw the stern frown on the face of the Chinese Customs official at the front of the line and stationed behind a glass window. He was very serious as he opened one suitcase after another, rummaging through everything that had been neatly packed. Passengers waited, then tried to reorganize their suitcases. No words were spoken. At that moment, I was no longer good with the idea of an axe!

I prayed and called on my God to help! How? I didn't know, but I knew that I desperately needed Him! I nervously waited my turn . . .

As I stepped up to the window, the Chinese Customs official checked my passport, intently looked at me, paused and then questioned, "Has anyone ever told you that you look exactly like Prime Minister Margaret Thatcher? You are free to go." Not a duffle bag was opened.

Only God could do that!

Ministry with SEND International

Darlene Armstrong served as a teaching intern in my office in her final year at Briercrest College in 1985. Little did either of us realize that sixteen years later we would be working together again, but this time around the world.

Darlene shares the reason for this incredible ministry with SEND International, in which we participated.

As with most mission organizations, there are more women than men in SEND. Each of these women plays an important role in helping SEND fulfill its mission, which is "to glorify God through establishing the church of Jesus Christ where it does not exist and serving it where it does exist."

Recognizing that SEND women are so valuable to the ministries God has given to SEND, our leadership requested that a study be conducted among them to determine if there are ways in which they can be further assisted in the fulfillment of the roles as members of SEND International. Jean was asked to lead the study and I have had the honor of assisting her in this.

Darlene and I began in Michigan, then Poland, Czech Republic and Slovenia. I then conducted the study in Alaska, while Darlene rejoined me for flights and ministries in Japan, Taiwan, Hong Kong, Spain and the Philippines.

Anywhere? Who would have thought?

Ministry with Japan Evangelical Missionary Association

Japan Evangelical Missionary Association, an organization that exists to network and equip disciples for Christ, plans an annual women's conference in Japan. SEND Japan also inspires and challenges their members attending their annual missionary conference. God blessed me with the privilege of participating in two consecutive conferences hosted by JEMA and sharing at one of the SEND conferences! To personally meet, interact and pray with so many missionaries serving in the beautiful country of Japan was pure joy!

Ministry with AVANT Ministries

During a ministry assignment at AVANT Headquarters in Kansas City, I had the privilege of participating in a weekend Missions Conference in Spain, attended the All-European conference in the Swiss Alps and Alton and I also spent a month in Mali, West Africa.

Harold and Kerry Peters and Alton and I flew to Bamako, the capital city of the Mali Republic, a city one thousand miles south of Timbuktu. We survived the Bamako traffic, were intrigued by their markets, tasted the rigors of the bush life and fell in love with the Malian people, who in their poverty were some of the most joyous people we had ever met! The hospitality of the missionaries was abundant and generous. They graciously shared their homes, time and ministries. I cannot think of words that adequately express the many ways we were enriched and blessed.

The first weekend I joined many missionaries and ex-pats in their annual Women's Retreat in one of Bamako's hotels. What a joy to minister to and be ministered to by these missionary women who had given their lives to Africa.

During the three remaining weeks in Mali, we enjoyed a blessed ministry in the bush stations, sharing truth with the wives of Malian pastors. Gary and Rita Mae became our caring hosts on those weekend ministries. My Bible lessons translated into Bambara became the basis for our study times together. Later these women would use the lessons as foundational materials for training and teaching the women believers in their congregations.

While preparing to go to Africa, I was advised to wear long dresses, as we would either stand or sit on low stools to teach. Because of the poverty, I was encouraged to buy appropriate clothing. I just bought a few long denim skirts and dresses. The Malian women, with their perfect ebony complexions, colorful dresses and matching head wraps, were simply beautiful! In comparison, I felt like a K-Mart Special!

No one can provide a personal glimpse of a typical weekend conference with Malian women like Ev Anderson. In a personal email received from her on May 21, 2005, she describes a weekend conference similar to the ones we experienced in the bush stations.

> The woman came on green machines, private cars and bus coaches. It is going to be a whole week away from their responsibilities at home, plus a week of no cooking, hours of catch up, visiting and more important than all, solid biblical teaching on subjects geared to address the daily problems women face here.
>
> They came with their best clothes in their small bags. The first day it poured rain. Rain isn't really conducive to camping outdoors, but every woman found a mat on which to sleep on the concrete floors in dormitories and classrooms. Maybe a little tight, but Malians love closeness. Later in the week they could sleep under the stars if they desired. No real mattresses were supplied. No one complained, even though they ached all over!
>
> Most of the younger women came with a nursing baby as well. Oh, and two of the woman gave birth during the week of camp! Wouldn't that be an extra stress for a Canadian Camp Director?

Later, the AVANT Missions Director in Argentina invited me to participate in their field conference in Buenos Aires.

I was totally intrigued by their vision and strategy for evangelism and discipleship, including ministry among the university students in Buenos Aires.

Ministry with S.I.M.

Wanting to encourage one of their own missionaries, Mount Olive Evangelical Free Church in Three Hills, Alberta, partnered with Denise, a SIM missionary, to fly me down to Bolivia. God gave me the joy of participating in a Missionary Women's Retreat in Cochabamba, Bolivia.

Denise worked at an international missionary kids' school and, through the students, developed strong relationships with many of the Bolivian moms in the school. Wanting to reach out to them and knowing how much Bolivians love teas, a tea for professional women was organized at a local hotel. Denise asked me to share my story in Spanish. One hundred and eighty women attended that tea and heard the gospel, many of them for the first time. One lady came to know the Lord that day and at least twenty other women asked for follow-up, including the mayor's wife, who indicated a desire to be part of a Bible Study. Only the Lord knows the real affect that tea had on the lives of Bolivian women, a group of people that Denise loves very dearly.

Ministry with the Evangelical Mennonite Church

Alvira Friesen of the Evangelical Mennonite Church graciously invited me to participate in their denominational conference in Mexico. This was one of those invitations where I answered with a definite "yes" even before praying about the invitation. Time with these wonderful people opened my eyes and my heart to what God is doing in and through the Mennonite people living in the northern provinces of Mexico.

Ministry with Central American Mission (Camino Global)

Harrison, Director of Mobilization for Central American Mission (now Camino Global) suggested something not achieved previously. He invited me to take my students who were enrolled in the "Missions Principles and Practices" course to Mexico. Shannon Irwin, my teaching intern and faculty assistant accompanied me.

We did it. We joined the students attending the CAM Bible Seminary in Puebla, Mexico. We ate together, debriefed together, participated in the student work on campus and served in student ministries in the local churches. When I taught classes on topics such as Language Learning and Cultural Adaptation, the students were immersed in it. When I taught on the Missionary Call, they interviewed the missionaries whose lives evidenced obedience to God's calling in their lives. Teaching Missions Principles on location takes on a totally different flavor. It was a great three weeks in Puebla, putting into practice lessons that would only have been theory on a Canadian campus.

North Africa

Each time I returned home after traveling, I was excited and would talk to any one who would listen! Of all the places I visited and the people I met, nothing quite compared with what I experienced in Morocco, a beautiful country with delicious Mediterranean food in Northwest Africa.

It was a Sunday morning as one by one we weaved in and around the open marketplace shops to meet in the "Big House,". This huge home with so much history now served as a secret meeting place for believers.

Gordon and Daphne served as skilled guides for those of us who were visiting Morocco. On that Lord's Day we were invited to join the believers who were secretly meeting to worship God.

From the minaret of a nearby mosque we heard the Muslim calls to prayer as we sang, prayed, read the Bible and heard the testimonies of local Moroccan Christians. Each one had a story—stories of how they had been imprisoned, beaten and persecuted for their faith. Following Christ was their only crime. They personally knew the high cost involved and the price they would pay when they crossed the line from a believer to a disciple.

In comparison, I had hardly begun to follow. In their presence I was among royalty. As we parted, the question was asked, "How can we pray for you?"

They responded, "Please don't pray for freedom. We have seen what freedom has done to America."

Building Personal Altars

BIOGRAPHIES HAVE ALWAYS INTRIGUED ME. SPECIFICALLY, MISSIONARY BIOGRAPHIES have challenged, inspired and at times convicted me. As I trace the lives of men and women in the Bible, I am fascinated as I identify with their weaknesses and desire to emulate their strengths. The stories of the Patriarchs of the Old Testament have compelled me to reflect on my own journey.

Abraham's story is one of many stories. Abraham built altars. Many of them were altars of worship. Genesis 12:8 records that Abraham built an altar at Bethel and worshipped there.

Chapter twenty-two of Genesis takes us to a place in the life of Abraham where he willingly built an altar of a different kind. It is the story of God asking Abraham to build an altar of relinquishment and to sacrifice his beloved son of promise on one of the mountains in the land of Moriah. Scripture always identifies the location of altars built, whether they be altars of worship or sacrifice.

During my spiritual journey, I have also, symbolically, built personal altars to worship God and discovered God anew. Exodus 20:24b (NLT) records the words of God to Moses saying, *"Build altars in the places where I remind you who I am, and I will come and bless you there."*

Amazing promise! No matter how difficult the altar, God promises to be there and assures to bless in that place. I have personally discovered that there has not been a time when building an altar of relinquishment where His presence was not evident or His blessing absent.

As I think about Abraham's altars, I recall the altars I have symbolically built. Many have been altars of worship, but there have also been altars of relinquishment, giving back what rightfully belongs to Him.

Altar of Vocation

As a believer in my late teens, the day came when I knew that I had to build an altar. Contentment filled my heart and I knew that my eternal destiny was secured. However, when it came to my vocation and career, I wanted my own way, to make my own plans and ignore God in the process. I believed that God wanted me in cross-cultural ministry, but I was not interested. While attending the fall missions conference on campus, I knew that I had to build an altar named Vocation and relinquish my plans to Him. As I have already written, it was that night that I scribbled my signature across a small card and committed to serve God "Anywhere, Anytime, Any Cost."

Altar of Singleness

Singleness was an issue that I knew that I had settle with God before I left Canada. My understanding of missions was that there were more single woman than single men on mission fields. I perceived that a decision to become a single missionary settled the likelihood of marriage, and a life alone was my only prospect. One night alone in my dormitory room, I built an altar and yielded my marital status to God, asking Him to give me joy and contentment as a future single missionary.

Little did I realize that one day I would build that altar a second time.

Altar of Location

I was very much aware that God had set me apart for a missionary career. I assumed that, as a missionary, I would go to Africa. Why, don't all missionaries go to Africa? Aren't the words "Africa" and "Missionary" synonymous terms? Many of my college friends were going to Africa. Was there anywhere else?

In the years that followed, God directed my steps with such clarity that I knew my location would not be Africa, but Panama, a small country that joined Central and South America. I built an altar of Location, relinquishing the location of ministry to Him. I never dreamt that I would have to build an identical altar several more times.

I felt like I was in kindergarten and just beginning to learn how trust God with my zip code.

Altar of Relinquishing My Health

One early morning before classes began, I was discipling a group of girls. The topic of the morning was "Lordship." I mentored them from Scripture and from personal experience, reminding them that our God is the Sovereign Lord, our forever Master and Guide. I concluded the class with the most incredibly foolish statement, saying, "I think I have learned all there is to learn about Lordship." I can't believe I said that! The girls went off to their classes and I went to the Campus Medical Clinic for my regular yearly physical with my family doctor. It was no big deal.

As a result of the routine checkup, the doctor discovered breast cancer.

The medical report stunned me and I became unglued! Major surgery for a mastectomy was scheduled. While waiting for surgery and before I went down to the Operating Room, I had another altar to build. This was an altar that I never once thought I would need to erect. The place was a room in the Moose Jaw Union Hospital. It was an altar relinquishing my body to Him.

God brought to my mind the words of the apostle Paul recorded in Romans 12:1–2, *"I beseech you therefore, brethren, by the mercies of God, that you present your bodies a living sacrifice, holy, acceptable to God, which is your reasonable service"* (NKJV). I prayed that if He would be most glorified by my body being riddled with cancer, then I would yield my body to Him for that purpose. As I went to surgery, my heart overflowed with God's peace and His words occupied my thoughts: *"Be still and know that I am God"* (Psalm 46:10, NKJV).

Leander Rempel, the Director of SEND International of Canada, heard of my upcoming surgery and began to fast and pray. Leander recalls,

I asked God to heal Jean for only one purpose, for the sake of missions at Briercrest, and for that matter, the rest of Canada. I was on one of my many trips to Western Canada. I was staying in the home of a godly Christian couple who lived just outside of Swift Current, Saskatchewan, when the news reached me of Jean's illness and upcoming surgery. I was out for my early morning jog and fellowship with the Lord when I became overwhelmed with the need to pray that God would heal her. I knelt right there in the snow bank beside the road and claimed the victory for the cause of Christ's Kingdom. Later in the morning but before she went to surgery, I called her to inform her that she wouldn't need surgery because she had been healed by the Great Physician.

God heard and answered Leander's supplication for the furtherance of the Kingdom. I am a cancer survivor only because of prayer and God's purposes. Therefore, I take very seriously my commitment to global missions.

An Altar of Releasing My Children

Releasing children for ministry never entered my mind. Sounds crazy, doesn't it? I had been an overseas missionary for nearly twenty years, had taught missions for twenty-four years, had served three years in a missions headquarters and served on mission boards. Why would releasing my children to overseas missionary service be anything but normal?

Baby dedications. How well I remember when Gil and I dedicated our two children to the Lord. We prayed that both of them would come to know Jesus at an early age and that they would live for Him and serve Him. No doubt many parents have prayed the same dedication prayer, asking God to bless their children in a ministry wherever He would lead. Then, when it happens and He answers, we are surprised. We have long forgotten the prayers we uttered at their baby dedications.

Babies grow up and years multiply.

Following Christ becomes really tough when He asks for everything, including my children. Then Jesus reminded me of His words recorded in Luke 14:26: *"If you want to be my disciple, you must hate everyone else by comparison—your father and mother, wife and children, brothers and sisters—yes, even your own life"* (NLT). Those are hard words from the Master! I knew that I could not call myself a Christ follower if I was not willing to release my children for ministry *anywhere!*

I was attending the annual missions conference happening on the Briercrest campus. As I listened to a missionary's report, the Holy Spirit spoke loudly, asking me to relinquish my children to Him. I couldn't wait for the missionary to finish his report. I ran out of the chapel and back to my office. I locked the door. I turned off the light. I hung my jacket over the door window. I had to be alone. There was another altar to build. I really believed that I had finished building all the altars of relinquishment, but God showed me otherwise. Tears flowed freely as I prayed and gave my children back to Him to serve Him where He would lead, knowing that His direction could be anywhere, absolutely anywhere—and yes, that there could be many tearful goodbyes at airports.

There will be more altars of worship to build, exalting Christ Jesus. I also know there will be more altars of relinquishment. How often I have reminded students and continually remind myself,

Discipleship is synonymous with Lordship and Lordship is synonymous with obedience.

Regardless of how many altars of relinquishment we build, we cannot ignore worship. Why? Because worship can't wait! One day Doug and Lynn, whose daughter Quinea was incredibly ill, beautifully illustrated for me this amazing truth and biblical principle!

Abraham built altars to worship at Bethel, and I, too, must find "my Bethel," a place and a time alone in His presence. I have lived long enough to know that it doesn't happen automatically; worship must be intentional. Although I have never met my Irish paternal grandmother, she modeled "Bethel worship" for me.

165

In the twilight years of Grandma's life, she lived in a small room at the end of the long house that belonged to her and Grandpa. A nephew, who had bought their farm home, cared for her as an aging widow. He gave her the small room at the end of the long house. Many decades after her death, on a Sunday afternoon while in Sligo, Ireland, I walked into her room. Her bed and chair were still there by the fireplace next to the bookshelf. On the shelf were books dating back one hundred years—books by D. L. Moody, Charles Spurgeon, R. A. Torrey and other great theologians. As I spent a few minutes alone in her room, I couldn't help but recall her words written to my dad many years before. She wrote, "I love my little room—I've made it my Bethel."

Murder Mystery and Motive Disclosed

WHEN I SET MY FEET ON THE TARMAC AT THE TOCUMEN AIRPORT FOR THE VERY FIRST time, the Republic of Panama boasted of less than a million, where mud huts with thatched roofs lined the villages of Panama's interior. Today, Panama, with its soaring skyline, now boasts the wealthiest economy in Latin America and has become the melting pot of races and cultures representing the entire globe. The reality of mass migrations is evident everywhere, as the entire world has become fluid. "The Bridge to the Americas" has now become "The Bridge to the World."

More than thirty years had passed since Gil's death, with the motive behind his murder still remaining a mystery.

A few years ago I had returned to Panama for a visit, and while there had the joy of fellowship with several graduates of Bethel Seminary. After eating a delicious meal prepared by Wynette, we just couldn't move back from the table! Hours were spent around the table reminiscing about the goodness of God in each of our lives. Then the conversation turned to the past and I heard a story totally unanticipated!

Two of the former Bethel Seminary students, Abilio and Gabriel, told the story. It seemed that the political leaders had intentions to make Panama a Communist State. A communist from South America was appointed as the leader of the Underground Communist Party. He was to target the university students, promoting and declaring the communist philosophy. If there were any that would hinder his progress, he was to take their lives.

The following letter received from Abilio adds another part of the story he began that afternoon around the dining room table.

Starting the year of 1970 and with the help of missionary brothers, Rev. Joe Jenkins and his son, Dr. Dan Jenkins, former Senator of Florida, I enrolled in Bethel Seminary, then located on the outskirts of Panama City.

I was young, filled with life and an overwhelming desire to learn. It was while studying at the seminary that I met Don Gilberto Reimer and his very distinguished wife, Juanita, their children, Glen and Betti Lou, and other missionaries who were seminary teachers. With the passage of time, I got to know Don Gilberto much better and my appreciation began to grow for him—not only as a teacher, advisor and friend, but also because of the many other great qualities that adorned him, especially his dedication to God and to his students.

He was a happy young man, with an amazing talent as a teacher, musician, preacher, evangelist and leader. He loved his family and his students, forming a quartet in the seminary, of which I became a part. We traveled to the different provinces of the country to sing and spread the message of the Lord.

After graduation from the seminary and having been doing God's work, it was thanks to Don Gilberto that I got my first secular job, working with a brother and friend, Mr. Peter Fast, at the Summer Institute of Linguistics in Panama City.

After some time here, I found out that Don Gilberto was teaching Bible Studies to college students at his own house, which was located very close to the University of Panama. All of this was happening at the time when Panama was under a military government led by Mr. Omar Torrijos in 1972 to 1973. Mr. Salvador Allende, former Chilean president and a consummated communist, had been ousted by Mr. Augusto Pinochet. Hundreds, if not thousands of communist sympathizers, in an attempt to flee depurations, immigrated to Panama under the guise of "college students." The new "students" became very active in our college's political scene and in short order, evolved into some of the strongest and most influential students on campus. Their influence grew so strong and wide that they were able to infiltrate our evangelism and missionary work.

One day one of these students, passing as a Christian, invited me to a meeting. I gladly accepted his invitation, thinking the meeting would be Christian education, but much to my chagrin, it turned out that it was more of a brain washing session than building and fulfillment itself. The session, I found, was devoted to anti-American sentiments ending in full-fledged hate. I now realized that this young man—supposedly Christian and who had invited me to this gathering—had very strong leftist, anti-American and anti-Semitist ideologies, so immediately I decided that I would neither befriend nor meet with this man again.

Sometime after this incident I received a very sad call where I was told of the disappearance of Don Gilberto Reimer and I ran to his home. His body was found days after I got the call.

On learning about Mr. Reimer's untimely decease, many unanswered questions invaded my mind. Truly, his demise affected me deeply, since I had grown to love him, not only as my friend and teacher, but also as my mentor. I could no longer contain my sentiments and, without a shred of shame, cried as I had never done before. I became very depressed because of the loss of this teacher whom God Himself had used so much in my own Christian growth.

Some years later I bumped into the same young man who had taken me to the "meeting" (whose name I omit for security reasons) and I asked him about his opinion on the murder of the missionary. He explained that it was a very good thing to have happened. Astounded, I asked him how could it ever be possible for him to think this way, especially as a professing Christian, to which he responded with a cryptic "They're looking for the other one" an underhanded reference to another missionary (whose name I will not give) and warned me to be "very careful."

It seems that the people involved in this sad business didn't like North American missionaries, who taught the Word of God to college students here in Panama. Years have gone by, but I have never been able to forget Don Gilberto. As a friend it seems as if everything just happened yesterday. One day I will be united with him forever.

Signed, Dr. A. F.

The Final Chapter is Yet to Be Written

SIX DECADES! SIX DECADES OF FOLLOWING JESUS, SOMETIMES TUCKED IN CLOSE behind Him, other times following at a distance, but always following, always longing to hear His voice.

Life without Christ as my Shepherd is a life difficult, if not impossible, to imagine. How would I have possibly maneuvered throughout life without Christ Jesus directing each step taken?

Six decades ago, I decided to follow Jesus. Following would never have happened if I had not first been wooed by Him, if He had not first created a spiritual vacuum in my soul and if He had not rescued and delivered me from the kingdom of darkness. He did. I believed. And I crossed over from one kingdom to another, the Kingdom of God. A kingdom is not a kingdom without a King. He is the Sovereign LORD, and I have become the daughter of the KING. This is called grace!

Times change and trends emerge. Globalization rooted in technology has taken our planet and transformed it into a global village. Our commitment to computers, emails, iPhones, iPods, text messages, Skype, Twitter and television have robbed us of time to think! Technology has also given us tools that six decades ago we did not have. I can't imagine writing my story on the first typewriter received as a gift from my dad. I am so grateful for a laptop with spell-checks, deletes, cut and paste features.

I have been glued to my laptop! Glued . . . while reflecting, recalling, recording the stories of life as a Christ follower. Glued . . . while contemplating the goodness of God, the grace He lavished and

His abiding presence as we walked together, my hand clasped in His.

As a teenager, I never thought there would be a day when my hair would be white. On my wedding day, it never entered my mind that I would be a young widow or that one day I would be a prairie girl with a Panamanian heart.

Now, as the decades have come and gone, I have arrived. How did I get here so fast? With each story I recalled and recorded, I saw the faithfulness of God operative in my life. I have the assurance that He who is the same yesterday, today and tomorrow will be faithful in the days yet to come. Why would I even think otherwise?

The decades have distanced me from my first public commitment to follow. Nevertheless, the decades have not distanced me from the One I decided to follow. On the contrary, God has taken me to a new level of following, trusting, loving Him. Joe Stowell says, "One of the rewards of following Christ is the simplicity and wonder it brings to life."[7] It is the wonder of God and for that reason, I keep being amazed!

These stories must not be kept to ourselves but declared to the next generation. It is not entirely a new notion. In Psalm 71:17–18 as King David recalled his youth, his prayer became,

O God, You have taught me from my youth;
And to this day I declare Your wondrous works.
Now also when I am old and grayheaded,
O God, do not forsake me,
Until I declare Your strength to this generation.
Your power to everyone who is to come. (NKJV)

I began to write especially for my grandchildren, then felt compelled to widen the horizon of readers to include many in this next generation. I am impressed with this generation that has so much potential, are so in love with Jesus and so uninterested in "stuff." My prayer and heart's desire is to showcase God, who overwhelmingly blesses us when we obey! When I think of how close I came to insisting on having my own way, following my own agenda and doing my own thing, I am so grateful to

---

[7] Joseph M. Stowell, *Following Christ* (Grand Rapids, MI: Zondervan, 1996), 22–23.

God, who loved me enough to ask for everything.

If you are still with me, have stuck with me through the stories of God's amazing grace, I encourage you to radically abandon everything to Christ. There is no better way! I trust my stories have communicated that.

Anytime?

A sense of entitlement has become pervasive in our culture. Somehow I was tempted to believe that when I received "the big brown envelope from the government," I also would receive the entitlement to do whatever, wherever and however I want. Getting older is a reality, and with every season I live within my present circumstances and limitations. Even so, as a Christ follower and regardless of my age, I cannot—dare not—live without purpose . . . anytime.

I am intrigued by Paul's one-line summary of King David's life. It is recorded in Acts 13:36 (NASB), *"For David, after he had served the purposes of God in his own generation, fell asleep, and was laid among his fathers."* In essence, this looked like David's purpose statement.

It is interesting that Paul did not say, "For David, after being incredibly busy, with his calendar cluttered, his days packed and being rushed off his feet, he fell asleep!" Terms like "busyness" and "purposes" are easily blurred and even confusing. God has been teaching me that my busy schedule is not a guarantee that I am fulfilling the purposes of God.

A Sudanese pastor who was speaking to his congregation of new immigrants to Canada asked, "Have you noticed how Canadians respond to the question, 'How are you?' Their answer is always, 'Busy.'"

A missionary friend recently home on furlough sat at our breakfast table. Tom Knight was amazed at how busy we all were. He concluded, "I can't help but believe that some North American Christians are going to arrive in heaven empty handed and out of breath!"

Living with God-given purpose is a daily challenge to commit to obedience. Over the years my goal has been to begin each day with God. Even before I lift my head off my pillow, I ask Him to direct my steps—the phone calls I should make, notes or text messages I should write and the people I should meet. At the end of the day, when I lay my head back on the pillow, I review the steps taken and am amazed!

As you can imagine, there are also days when I quickly hop out of bed without even a thought of including Him in my plans, doing everything on my own just because I was in too much of a hurry to ask.

I only get one generation. There are no more. There are now more years behind than before me. Not all finish well. One only has to observe how some whose lives are recorded in the Bible started well and finished poorly. I am not home yet. Apart from Him I can do nothing, and finishing well is only by His grace.

Recalling, remembering and recording the stories of God's goodness, provision and direction in my life has brought to mind threads running through the tapestry of my life.

One thread is the blessing of the Church. We did not travel the journey alone, but fellow Christ followers have been present to bless, encourage and give guidance. Their stories would fill another book. I thank God for the electrician and his wife from Berne, Indiana, who gave up their well earned vacation to completely rewire the Farm. I'm thankful for Paul and Pauline, who risked being stopped at customs in London as they brought a water heater to Panama (so that we could have hot showers) and who chose to take their furlough in England so that we could have their home while on our furlough. These couples represent many who followed in their footsteps and blessed in countless tangible ways. I have said it before and it bears repeating, I will never cease to be thankful for the body of Christ. It is impossible to love Jesus and not His Bride.

Another common thread throughout is the reality of God's provision in gifting each of His children with spiritual gifts. I thank God for giving me a gift and love for teaching. Although my zip code has changed many times down through the years, God has always provided opportunities to teach His Word and mentor young women. A podium isn't always necessary. Sometimes a booth at Ricky's restaurant on Country Hills Boulevard works just fine.

The greatest and most amazing gift of all is that God the Holy Spirit lives within! I can do absolutely nothing apart from the One who abides in this temple of clay. Paul reminds us in 2 Corinthians 4:7, *"We have this treasure in jars of clay to show that this all-surpassing power is from God and not from us"* (NIV). How incredibly grateful I am for the Treasure within.

At the end of the day all I am is just an ordinary fragile temporary clay pot! That's it, nothing more.

How amazing that God, the Creator of Universe who dwells IN me, is the ONE who empowers, enables and anoints me. The fact that it is Christ in me, the hope of glory is a powerful thought that Paul records in Colossians 1:27.

If anything of lasting value has been accomplished through my life, it has been accomplished only through the power of the Holy Spirit who dwells within. To Him be all the glory!

Six decades have passed since I sang this simple but incredibly profound chorus: "I have decided to follow Jesus, no turning back, no turning back. Though none go with me, yet still I will follow, no turning back." It expressed the intent and devotion of a teenager who had no idea what following Jesus would look like.

I am still following and I love Him too much to turn back now.

Within the first year of widowhood, I met Rev. Elwyn Davies, International Director of Bible Christian Union, who was visiting on the Briercrest Campus. He blessed, encouraged and comforted me. During our time together, he told me of Mrs. Hector McMillan, the wife of martyred Congo missionary Hector McMillan.

He related how, during her travels as a new widow, young women would ask her this question: "If you had known how far the Lord would have taken you, would you have accepted Hector's proposal to be his wife?"

Her response was always: "I still don't know how far." She would then challenge them with these words, "Young people, you may have to go further than you think."

Elwyn Davies was inspired with the words of this new widow, spoken only three months after her husband's martyrdom, and penned, "How Far, LORD?"

How far, Lord?

Until the miles are meaningless
And the well-loved scenes are lost;
'Till Hearts are filled with weariness
And men say, " 'Tis too great a cost."
How can I take the long road
Which leads o'er hill and dale
And drink the cup of loneliness
Right up to death's dark vale?
Is this what Thou dost ask of me?
Is this my share of Calvary?
Until the miles are meaningless
And the well-loved scenes are lost,
I'll walk with Thee, O Savior blest
Till the last great range is crossed,
THAT FAR, LORD!

I was so impressed with The words of Elwyn Davie's poem that I asked permission to use it in my conference speaking. And now, I ask myself…

How many more altars? How many more miles? How far? I don't know. However, I do know that life has been a great God-adventure, and it all began when I radically abandoned everything to Him. He has blessed me above and beyond!

However, blessings are not the rationale for yielding everything to Him. No one describes the purpose and motivation for total surrender more eloquently than well-known hymn writer Isaac Watts when he penned,

When I survey the wondrous cross, on which the Prince of glory died.
Were the whole realm of nature mine,
That were a present far too small;
His love so amazing, so divine
Demands my soul, my life, my all!

The cost? Jesus paid it all. The price He paid for me demands everything—my soul, my life, my all! That is exactly why I abandon all to Him. He alone is worthy. Six decades of following have taught me that it is not only safe but glorious to trust God with my zip code!

God still has the pen. He is still writing. The last chapter has yet to be written.

Epilogue

YEARS HAVE PASSED SINCE THE BEGINNING OF THIS STORY. LIFE HAS A WAY OF STRETCHING and expanding our horizons. There are more family members around our dining room table, Christmas gifts include more grandchildren and great grandchildren, and in reality, the epilogue is never completed.

This story began with a summary of my Irish heritage. What was written was all I knew, that is, until recently when I discovered I had an Irish cousin living in Alberta. Cousins Ray and Ina Gillespi invited me to visit Ireland with them. What joy to meet cousins for the first time, spend time in my Grandma Gillespi's home and visit the home where my dad was raised. *Anywhere?* God did it!

More than fifty years have passed since Gil and I were married and nearly forty years since his Home-going. I continue to be very grateful for fifty-one years as a member of the Reimer family. What joyous privilege to be counted as one of the Penner Cousins, who for nearly sixty years have met annually to celebrate their heritage.

Thirty-five years ago, I became part of another family when I married Alton Barsness. Alton's wife Janet passed away at age thirty-one, leaving Alton a widower and the father of three children ages nine, five and three. Alton remained single for fifteen years, raising Carol Elaine, Berva Ann and Duane Neil on his own. On our wedding day, we became a blended family of five.

Carol and Ray Wall make their home in Rosebud, Alberta where Ray pastors the Covenant Church. They thank God for two grown sons, Scott and Trent.

Scott married Darlene Zondervan, and they are blessed with three children: Haley, Brandon and Norah, living in Kitchener, Ontario, while studying at the university. Trent married Jenni Duke and they are blessed with two children, Ryker and Brynlee. They make their home in Estevan, Saskatchewan.

Berva married Paul Hinderager, and they are successful ranchers and have two grown sons, Jess and Eric. Jess married Dani Fleming, and they are blessed with two children: Kale Owen and Nora Grace. They live near Vaughn, Montana.

Duane married Connie Fleck, and they are blessed with two children: Joy Janet and Luke Robert. They live on the family farm at Frontier, Saskatchewan.

Glen and his family make their home in Saskatchewan, where both he and his wife are educators. They have blessed us with three young adult grandsons, Greg, Mark and Joel, who all are university students.

Betts and her family make their home in Philadelphia. Their daughter, Dallas, a dental hygienist is married to Rob Bailey, an attorney. Their son, Dalton, is a student at Lancaster Bible College and serves as a Pastor of Worship.

We have grateful hearts that all our children are Christ followers. This is called Grace!

This postscript provides an update on our family, bringing closure to several months of writing, recording the countless blessings of God as together we travelled the path assigned by Him.

Anywhere, Anytime, Any Cost

Signed ....

Date ....